indeed. In this book, Huy tackles the question of AI, and if anyone is qualified to do that, it's him. So: a must-read for anyone who wants a true insight into our future world and way of working, as well as living.

Caroline Stockmann, Non-Executive Director, Bank of England

Huy Nguyen Trieu's The AI-fication of Jobs is a must-read for anyone navigating today's world of work and innovation. With unmatched insights and his lifelong dedication to adult education, Huy offers a roadmap for understanding the profound impacts of AI on jobs and careers. This book isn't just a guide — it's a reference for future leaders and a must-have for anyone serious about shaping the future. Get ready to rethink, realign, and redefine your career with Huy's exceptional wisdom at your side.

Michael O'Loughlin, Founder, OLOUGHLIN.io

W0013444

The AI-fication of Jobs
Preparing Ourselves for the Future of Work

By

Huy Nguyen Trieu

THE
AI-FICATION
OF JOBS

PREPARING OURSELVES
FOR THE FUTURE OF WORK

HUY NGUYEN TRIEU

Published by *CFTE – Centre for Finance, Technology and Entrepreneurship*
courses.cfte.education

CFTE Centre for Finance, Technology and Entrepreneurship

Name: Nguyen Trieu, Huy, author.

Title: The AI-fication of Jobs: Preparing Ourselves for the Future of Work / Huy Nguyen Trieu

Other titles: Ai-fication, Aification

Description: London, CFTE, 2024

Identifiers: ISBN 978-1-0685567-3-9 (print) | ISBN 978-1-0685567-0-8 (limited edition print) | ISBN 978-1-0685567-2-2 (ebook) | ISBN 978-1-0685567-1-5 (hardcover)

Subjects: LCSH: Artificial intelligence — Social aspects. | Artificial intelligence — Educational applications. | Labor — Effect of technological innovations on. | Education — Effect of technological innovations on.

Cover design: Rhea Singhania
Book Illustrations: Rhea Singhania

While the author has made every effort to provide accurate estimates for data figures at the time of publication, neither the publisher nor the author assumes any responsibility for errors or for changes that occur after publication or differences in historical estimates. Further, the publisher and author do not have any control over and does not assume any responsibility for third-party websites or their content. Every statistic stated is based on multiple sources and may differ to other estimates.

To Tram Anh, without whom my world wouldn't exist

To my wonderfully special daughters

To my family

AI-fication of jobs?
AI-ification of jobs?
AI-isation of jobs?
AI-tion of jobs?

What's in a name?
That which we call a rose, by any other word
would smell as sweet.
Romeo and Juliet

Acknowledgements

It's often said that an article or blog post captures a fleeting thought or moment, while a book brings together a lifetime of experiences and insights.

This certainly proved true for me while writing *The AI-fication of Jobs*. The process was enriched by memories and lessons from countless discussions I've had over the years.

While it's impossible to individually thank every person who has helped shape my thinking, taught me something new, or offered a fresh perspective, I want to express my deepest gratitude to all those with whom I've had the pleasure to share time. Your contributions have helped make me who I am today.

There are a few people I would like to acknowledge personally, as their contributions have profoundly impacted this book. First and foremost, a very big thank you to Janos Barberis, CEO of Supercharger Ventures. His unique blend of deep thinking and entrepreneurial skills has significantly shaped my work at CFTE and greatly influenced my ideas in general.

A very big thank you to the "Fintech family", that global ecosystem of do-ers and thinkers who meet at events like the Singapore Fintech Festival, Point Zero in Zurich, and 24 Fintech in Riyadh. Over the last eight years, this diverse and international community has immensely enriched my perspective.

The team at CFTE has been a crucial pillar in the creation of this book. Over the past seven years, we have united the worlds of education, technology, and finance, laying the foundation for the insights and experiences that have shaped this work. Thank you to everyone at CFTE for continually pushing our thinking forward.

Within the team, I must particularly acknowledge the truly superb work of Rhea Singhania in CFTE's Singapore office. Although she joined the team just nine months ago as a young graduate, this book wouldn't have been possible without her. Rhea served as my sparring partner, conducted complex research, created the illustrations, and played a significant role in bringing the book to completion. I'm continually amazed by the new generation, and Rhea exemplifies the "Supercharged Professional" you'll read about later in the book.

I would also like to thank my family, whose constant support — whether for this book or in life — is the foundation on which I build everything. To my parents, Tram Anh's parents, Khang, Thanh Tuyen and their beautiful children, and Thanh Thuy, *a different artist,* who has helped me see the world with greater compassion.

And of course, this book would never have been possible without Tram Anh, my wife and partner in both life and business. Entrepreneurship is hard, with very high highs and very low lows, and being a couple in entrepreneurship doesn't make it easier, especially for the one who brings stability to the family. Thank you Tram Anh, without whom my world wouldn't exist.

And finally, big hugs to our smart, curious, and caring daughters, who have been the first supporters and the most critical audience of this book!

Table of Contents

Preface

Without AI, this book wouldn't exist.

Don't worry, I don't mean it was written by ChatGPT. *At least, not all of it.*

Over the last 15 years, I've started many book projects but never finished them. The first was during the global financial crisis, titled *Diary of (Un)-expected Events*.

It was a macroeconomic analysis of the crisis and its far-reaching consequences — rising inequalities, social tensions, and populism. I should have written it, my thesis ended being true.

But this time, I did finish the book — and it's thanks to AI.

First, AI helped me work 5 times faster than before and gave me something an entrepreneur never has – time. By speeding up the research and writing process, it made me a **Supercharged Professional** — a concept we'll explore further in the book.

Secondly, AI is a topic that has been close to my heart since 2018, when I co-created the AI in Finance certification. Since then, I've been deeply involved in the AI space, exploring its diverse forms and applications up close. I believe that my insights into AI and the future of work can **help others** better understand how to adapt, thrive, and lead in this rapidly changing world.

This book is written for three audiences:

- **Policymakers and industry leaders** who have the power to shape the future.
  With great power comes great responsibility.

- **Professionals, students, and anyone curious about the future of work.**
  The future belongs to those who prepare for it today.

- **Everyone who wants to be an active participant in the AI revolution, not just a spectator.**
  Be the change that you wish to see in the world.

Wherever you are, and whatever brings you to this book, I thank you for joining me in this exploration of **The AI-fication of Jobs**.

Through this journey, we will discuss the trends shaping the future of work, and more importantly, how we can take control of AI's impact. My ambition for this book is to spark meaningful discussions and help readers take action.

I hope this book inspires you to take part in shaping the future of AI and work.

If you'd like to continue the conversation, feel free to connect with me on LinkedIn — mention **AI-fication** in your message.

Who wrote this book?

I hope you'll enjoy this book, and it shouldn't matter who wrote it, whether it's me or someone else. After all, authors have used ghostwriters for centuries – even Pythagoras had his followers write down his teachings.

But today, in the age of AI, I'm sure you were not thinking about whether I used a ghostwriter. The real question is: **was this book written by an AI?**

Would it change your experience if I told you I spent ten months researching, thinking deeply, and revising five different versions? You could almost picture me sitting in front of my computer, surrounded by research notes, slowly writing each chapter.

Or would you view it differently if I told you ChatGPT generated the outline, text, and illustrations in just 92 seconds – while I was commuting in the London tube?

Which version would you value more? Which one would you trust? Could you even tell the difference?

These are the fascinating questions we now face, and there's no doubt this is the world we're entering.

So, to answer the original question: who wrote this book? It was a team effort, made up of three key people, sorry, 3 members:

- Myself, Huy, the human author
- Rhea Singhania, also human, an analyst at CFTE
- ChatGPT, the AI tool you're already familiar with

I did most of the thinking, drawing on my experience in entrepreneurship, technology, and academia. Rhea was an excellent sounding board, offering feedback, supporting with research and contributing her beautiful illustrations. And

ChatGPT? It played the critical role of research assistant and editor.

As of 2024, I believe very few people could have written this book because it's based on my unique thinking and experience connecting different worlds — entrepreneurship, technology, business models, and business.

And no AI is close to writing a book like this **today**. But I believe that in a few years, AI will be capable of generating original thinking that would surpass what I've done here.

So yes, it's a human who wrote this book. And because of that, there may be flaws and imperfections — but this is exactly what makes it valuable!

Happy reading!

Introduction

"We can be blind to the obvious, and we are also blind to our blindness. When confronted with large numbers, our minds struggle to process them, and they lose their meaning."

Daniel Kahneman, Thinking, Fast and Slow

The IMF forecasts that **60% of jobs in developed economies will be heavily impacted by AI**. In half of these cases, AI will augment workers and increase productivity. In the other half, it is likely to replace existing tasks, leading to lower wages, reduced demand for workers, and un-employment.

Goldman Sachs predicts that **AI could replace 300 million jobs globally.**

When we hear numbers like "60%" or "300 million", it's easy to lose sight of what they mean. Large numbers in reports sound analytical and distant, but they mask the human impact they represent. These figures can numb us to what is truly happening.

Let's put things in perspective.

You likely remember the global subprime crisis that led the entire world into a major recession. It may have impacted you personally, or someone close to you.

Governments borrowed trillions — yes, trillions — of dollars to stabilise the economy. Even then, it took a decade for major economies to regain their footing.

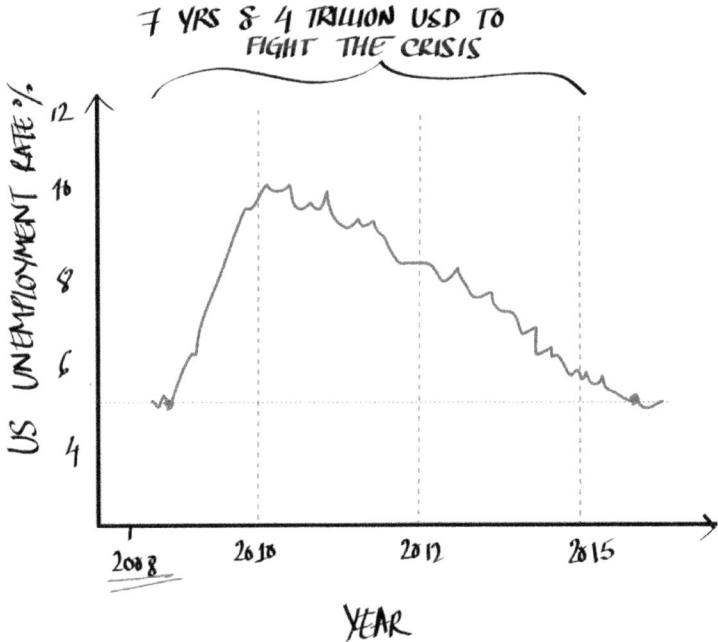

7 YRS & 4 TRILLION USD TO FIGHT THE CRISIS

US UNEMPLOYMENT RATE %

Unemployment skyrocketed. In the US, the rate doubled from 5% in 2008 to 10% within two years. It took seven years and $4 trillion in quantitative easing to recover those jobs.

Globally, 20 million jobs were lost during the biggest economic crisis in a century.

Now, consider this: AI could impact jobs on a scale **ten times greater** than that crisis.

It doesn't make sense:

- Either the IMF, World Bank, Goldman Sachs, and others are correct, and every politician in every country should treat this as their top priority.
- Or they are wrong, and we need to understand why.

At this point, you might think this book is another **doom-and-gloom narrative** about AI taking over jobs. I assure you, **it is not**!

The AI-fication of Jobs is a structured analysis of AI's impact on employment. More importantly, it's an invitation for you, Reader, to challenge our current, often limited, thinking on this crucial topic and to become an active participant in this significant transformation.

I'm sure you remember the first time you encountered Generative AI. Maybe a colleague excitedly showed you how to use ChatGPT, or perhaps you saw an intriguing LinkedIn post.

For me, it was a 2021 article in the *MIT Technology Review* that described what Open AI's GPT-3 could do. I was blown away by how it could craft such a magical story:

Bizarre prompt from researcher:

In a shocking finding, scientists discovered a herd of unicorns living in a remote, previously unexplored valley in the Andes Mountains. Even more surprising to the researchers was the fact that the unicorns spoke perfect English.

Story invented by machine:

They also were found to have perfectly coiffed hair, and wore what appeared to be Dior makeup.
"We were shocked to discover the unicorns," said anthropologist Daniel St. Maurice. "They were like nothing we had ever seen before. We had heard legends of the unicorns, but never thought they actually existed."

When ChatGPT was launched in November 2022, I was **amazed**. And then **scared**.

> Wanted to have your views. What do you think of ChatGPT? 15:29 ✓✓

> Not tried it directly myself but whatever I see on their site is impressive. More broadly, Nat lang processing and generation are probably some of the most successful uses of AI right now 15:33

> My belief is that too often, AI is being used to solve problems that can be solved in another way, slightly better 15:34

> We tried it and I'm very scared actually. 15:34 ✓✓

> This kind of stuff changes that - it starts solving problems that no automated alternative does as well 15:34

> Because 1, a lot of jobs can now be replaced and 2, there is no ethics embedded 15:35 ✓✓

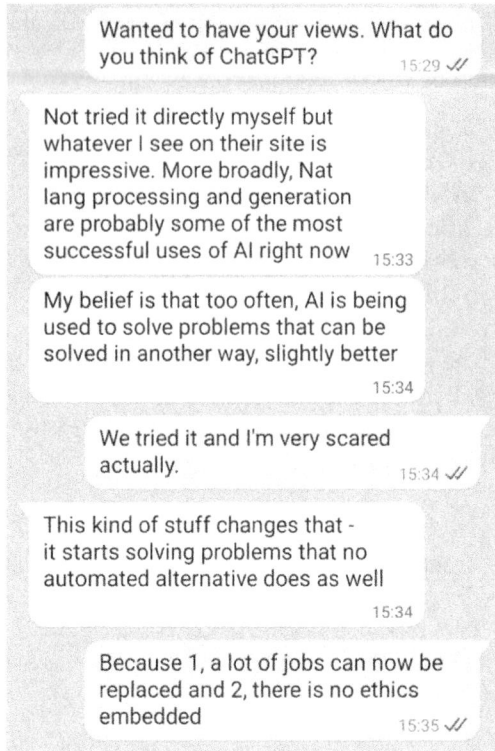

Whatsapp I shared with a friend and AI expert a few days after the launch of ChatGPT

This is unusual for me. I'm an entrepreneur — and therefore an optimist!

I'm far from a technophobe, too. After graduating from MIT, I was CEO of a tech company. I experienced the Internet revolution first-hand, even creating the equivalent of LinkedIn five years before LinkedIn existed. (I could write an entire book about timing in startups...)

In 2017, Tram Anh and I founded the Centre for Finance, Technology and Entrepreneurship, with the goal of providing everyone with the knowledge to thrive in a tech-driven world.

In 2018, I became Programme Director for the first AI certification in finance, driven by the belief that "AI is the single most important technology impacting our industry."

So, if anything, I should be thrilled about the latest developments in Generative AI. And I am — **if we manage it properly.**

What scares me about AI is how society is being lured into its embrace, much like sailors drawn to the sirens' song. We are captivated by its promise, rushing ahead without considering the consequences.

We're so focused on AI's promise that we overlook its potential negative impacts, especially on employment and society. This blind rush leaves us unprepared for the profound changes AI is bringing.

AI has the potential to be an incredible **force for transformation** — one that could bring greater prosperity, create better jobs, and solve problems we've never been able to tackle.

But it can only happen if we, as individuals, leaders, and society, actively engage in the discussion. As I like to say, *AI is too important to be left to the technologists.*

Before I embarked on this book, my thoughts on AI's impact on jobs were as follows:

- AI capabilities are reaching a point where they are good enough to replace many human tasks, leading to job destruction.
- A small number of people will thrive by leveraging AI.
- Some new jobs will be created, but it's difficult to predict which ones.

Since 2023, we've already seen some of this happening. Some companies have replaced customer service agents or translators with AI, while others, like ours, have become more productive by integrating AI. Meanwhile, new roles — like prompt engineers and AI fashion model creators — have emerged.

These are interesting developments, but they remain anecdotal, hinting at what might come.

Most research on AI's impact on jobs focuses on macro numbers, projecting the millions of jobs potentially affected, or take a skill-based approach, breaking down occupations into tasks to see which are most susceptible to automation.

Generally, the research points to the following:

- AI will have a significant impact on the majority of jobs.
- Hundreds of millions of people, especially those in routine and repetitive tasks, could be negatively affected.
- New jobs will be created, though we don't yet know which ones.
- By breaking down job roles into tasks, we can rank the jobs most likely to be impacted.
- White-collar jobs in developed economies will be disproportionately affected.

Recognising this, many leaders have responded by saying, **"We need to upskill and reskill people."** As the co-founder of an education platform that does just that, I wholeheartedly agree.

However, with our current understanding of how AI is impacting jobs, our efforts will be **minuscule** at best, because of a very simple reason:

We do not understand how AI transforms jobs

In other words, while we can observe and anticipate some macro effects — like job displacement or the creation of new roles — we do not know what are the underlying mechanisms of this transformation.

This is akin to treating a feverish child with paracetamol (treating the symptom) versus giving her antibiotics (treating the cause).

Why is it hard to understand AI's impact on jobs? It's because we're approaching it from a limited perspective: that of the *incumbent* — the worker whose role may change or disappear. While it's natural to focus on how people are affected, this view actually restricts our understanding. It's like trying to predict the future of the Telecom industry from Nokia's point of view, without factoring in the disruptive potential of Apple's iPhone.

I'm not suggesting that humans are Nokia and AI is the iPhone. What I'm saying is that, when it comes to the future of jobs, we have the *incumbent* (humans) and the *disruptor* (AI).

To truly understand what's ahead, we need to shift our perspective and examine it from the disruptor's point of view — AI's perspective — to fully grasp the changes on the horizon.

When we make this shift, we start to see the bigger picture. We can anticipate the very powerful trends which are already starting to transform the way we work :

- **Mass Displacement**: AI automating tasks and leading to significant workforce changes.
- **Supercharged Professionals**: Workers leveraging AI to become more productive and innovative.
- **Creative Disruptors**: AI enabling new industries and small teams to have an outsized impact.

By shifting our perspective from the incumbent's view to the disruptor's standpoint, we can leverage innovation models and structured frameworks that are effective in predicting future trends. This approach helps us alleviate confusion, and structures our thinking to anticipate changes, mitigate risks, and fully leverage AI's benefits.

AI has the potential to be an **incredible force for good**, one that can create better jobs, drive greater prosperity, and solve problems we've struggled with for generations. But to realise this potential, we need to **actively engage** — as individuals, leaders, and societies.

If you're ready to explore how AI is transforming jobs and what you can do about it, this book is for you.

The AI-fication of Jobs is organised in five chapters:

- **Looking Back**: A review of how technological innovations, from the steam engine to the Internet, have historically impacted jobs.
- **Exploring the Debate**: Different schools of thought on AI's impact — will it follow historical patterns or is it uniquely transformative?
- **Decoding Innovation**: Introduction of the **CDE model**, a framework that helps make sense of technology shifts and predict trends.

- **AI and Jobs**: Application of the **CDE model** to understand the mechanisms behind AI's impact on employment.
- **Shaping the Future**: Strategies for individuals, businesses, and policymakers to thrive in an AI-driven world.

By the end of this book, I hope you'll feel better prepared to navigate the future of work and play an active role in building a future of collective abundance.

Let's begin this journey together.

Part I:

What Three Industrial Revolutions Teach Us About Jobs

Lessons from the steam engine, electricity, and the Internet

Fear and Hope: What Unites Technology Revolutions

"I am convinced that the substitution of machinery for human labour is often very injurious to the interests of the class of labourers… [It] may increase the net revenue of the country, and at the same time render the population redundant"

David Ricardo, *third edition of Political Economy and Taxation, 1821*

The First Industrial Revolution: 50 times more cotton, new industries, but fewer artisans.

Luddite, *noun.*

(derogatory) A person opposed to new technology or ways of working.

(historical) a member of any of the bands of English workers who destroyed machinery, especially in cotton and woollen mills, that they believed was threatening their jobs (1811–16).

Fighting cheaper and faster machines

Imagine being a skilled weaver in the early 19th century. For years, you've woven fabrics by hand in your small, home-based workshop, a master of your craft. Your work isn't glamorous, but it's valued. You earn 15 to 20 shillings a week — a modest income, but enough to support your family and hold a respectable place in your community. Although your income isn't high, your skill is in demand, and there's pride in knowing that your hands bring each piece of cloth to life.

But as the Industrial Revolution gathers pace, something begins to change. Machines such as the power loom and the wide-frame knitting machine appear in factories. These machines can do the work that once took hours, faster, and at a fraction of the cost. The beautiful fabrics you spend hours creating by hand are now being woven by machines — machines that can produce as much as 24 yards of cloth per day, six times more than you could ever weave in the same time. Suddenly, the skills that once secured your livelihood are becoming irrelevant.

At the same time, economic conditions are worsening. The ongoing Napoleonic Wars have disrupted trade, led to shortages, and driven up food prices, making it even harder to sell traditional, handmade textiles. Demand for your craft dwindles, and so does your income. You used to earn 15 to 20 shillings a week, but now, as machines take over, you're making just 6 to 8 shillings — the same wage as unskilled factory workers. The sharp drop of over 60% in your income plunges you into poverty, and you wonder how long you can continue to provide for your family.

It's not just you. Across Nottinghamshire, Yorkshire, and Lancashire, thousands of skilled artisans are facing the same struggle. Once the backbone of England's textile economy, these weavers are seeing their livelihoods and status slip away as machines take over. It's in this desperate context that the Luddite movement begins.

A desperate struggle to keep their jobs

The Luddites, named after the mythical figure Ned Ludd, weren't backward-thinking rioters, as history sometimes portrays them. They were skilled artisans who had been pushed to the brink. They saw machines not as tools of progress, but as competitors. From 1811 to 1816, they took matters into their own hands, organising raids to break into factories and smash the very machines they believed were stealing their jobs.

In Nottinghamshire alone, up to 1,000 Luddites participated in machine-breaking raids in a single year. Across the country, estimates suggest that as many as 12,000 workers were involved in Luddite activities. Armed with hammers and other simple tools, they would target the factories most responsible for undermining their livelihoods, hoping to send a message to factory owners and the government.

But the government's response was swift and brutal. The British government saw the Luddite movement as a serious threat to social order. In 1812, the Frame Breaking Act was passed, making machine-breaking a capital offence. By 1813, 14 Luddites were hanged in York, with others sentenced to transportation to penal colonies in Australia. By 1816, the movement had been crushed, leaving the Luddites either forced into low-paying factory jobs or lost to poverty.

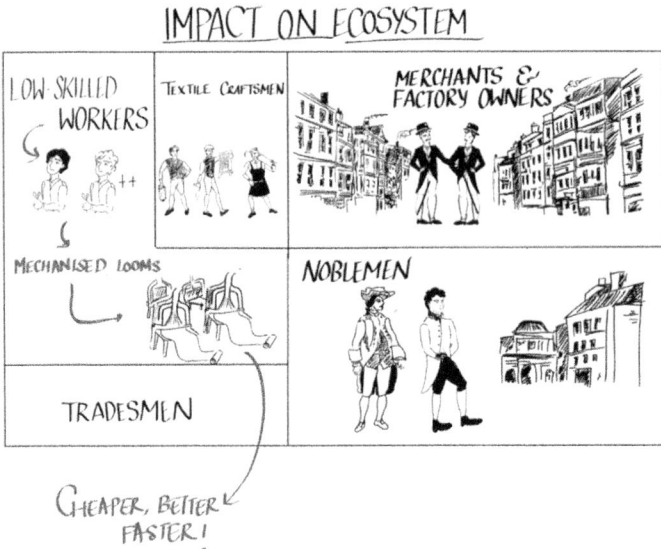

IMPACT ON ECOSYSTEM

The story didn't end well for the Luddites. Their fears materialised as they had anticipated, resulting in loss of employment, loss of status, and a need to find jobs that paid significantly less. By 1830, only around 50,000 handloom weavers remained from the 250,000 to 300,000 employed in the early 1800s. The traditional way of life they had fought so hard to protect had largely disappeared.

But the first Industrial Revolution was positive for society

However, this is not the whole story. While the Luddites and other artisans suffered, society as a whole experienced dramatic economic growth. Mechanisation revolutionised textile production. A skilled weaver could produce around 3 to 4 yards of cloth per day, while power looms could weave up to 24 yards per day — a six-fold increase in productivity. Cotton production soared from 52 million pounds in 1800 to 2.5 billion pounds by 1850, a fifty-fold increase.

As factories proliferated, overall employment in the textile industry actually increased. By 1850, around 600,000 to 700,000 people were employed in textile factories, including women and children, though often with much lower wages than the skilled artisans they replaced. While textile production was once slow and labour-intensive, mechanisation allowed Britain to increase its textile exports dramatically — from 15-20% of British exports in 1800 to nearly 40% by the 1830s — cementing its position as the world's leading economic power.

Although the story ended poorly for the Luddites, for society at large, mechanisation brought new industries, more jobs, and unprecedented economic growth. The costs were real, especially for artisans, but the long-term gains for the economy were undeniable.

Will AI Create Modern-Day Luddites?

Can we draw similar parallels between AI and the disruptions of the Industrial Revolution? As new technologies emerge that can do the same tasks as humans but cheaper, faster, and more efficiently, there are growing concerns that some people will inevitably be left behind. This fear is already

35

evident in industries like entertainment, where Hollywood writers recently went on strike, demanding protections against the use of generative AI.

Some of these writers have compared themselves to modern-day Luddites. While the original Luddites broke machines in an attempt to save their jobs, these skilled professionals didn't resort to smashing computers but instead organised strikes, aiming to protect their livelihoods from AI. The result? They successfully negotiated limits on the use of generative AI in screenwriting, ensuring that human creativity would still have a place in the industry.

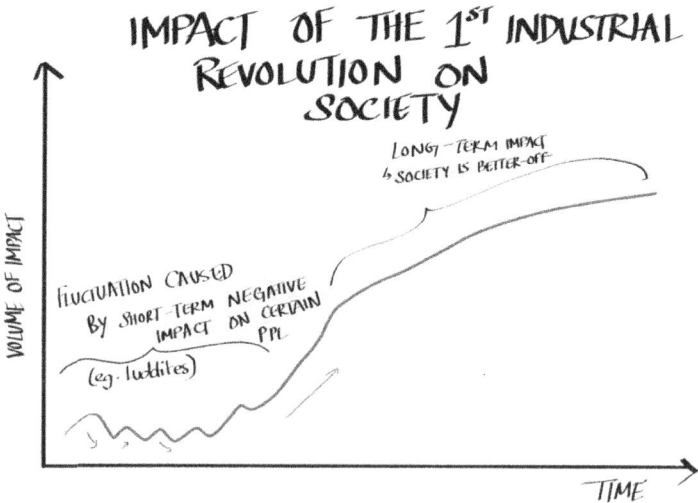

IMPACT OF THE 1ˢᵗ INDUSTRIAL REVOLUTION ON SOCIETY

LONG-TERM IMPACT
↳ SOCIETY IS BETTER-OFF

VOLUME OF IMPACT

FLUCTUATION CAUSED
BY SHORT-TERM NEGATIVE
IMPACT ON CERTAIN PPL
(e.g. luddites)

TIME

Just as the Luddites feared the rise of machines, these writers and many others worry about a future where AI might replace skilled workers across industries. The conclusion from the Luddite story is clear: some people lost out, but overall, society adapted and grew. The mechanisation of the 19th century created new industries, more jobs, and ultimately led to economic growth, even if it came at a steep cost for certain workers.

The question now is: will it be the same with AI? In my conversations with people around the world, there seems to be a general sense that **while some may be displaced, AI could lead to new opportunities**, industries, and economic growth —just as the Luddites' world transformed with mechanisation. But will it really turn out that way?

Summary of the First Industrial Revolution

Description: Spanning from the late 18th century to the early 19th century, started in Great Britain. This period marked the transition from manual production methods to mechanised factory systems, driven by innovations such as the steam engine and mechanised textile manufacturing.

Main Impact on Employment:

- Shift from agricultural to industrial employment, with millions moving to urban areas to work in factories. For instance, by 1851, over 50% of Britain's population lived in urban areas, compared to just 20% in 1750.

- Significant growth in factory-based jobs: Textile production increased dramatically, with mechanised cotton mills employing thousands of workers who previously would have worked in workshops or on farms.

Those Who Benefited:

- **Skilled machine operators**: Workers who could operate and maintain the new machines earned relatively higher wages than unskilled labourers.

Those Who Were Left Behind:

- **Craftsmen and Artisans**: Skilled workers, like weavers and blacksmiths, were displaced by factories that mass-produced goods more quickly and cheaply, reducing demand for handmade items.
- **Agricultural Workers**: Mechanisation, such as the threshing machine, reduced the need for farm labour, pushing many rural workers to cities in search of factory jobs.

Impact on Society:

- **Urbanisation**: The population of cities like Manchester grew rapidly, from 25,000 in 1771 to over 300,000 by 1851.

- **Working conditions**: Long working hours, child labour, and dangerous conditions were common, leading to social unrest and the eventual rise of labour movements.

Impact on Economy:

- **Economic Growth**: Britain's GDP grew quickly, with an annual growth rate of about 2% during the early 19th century, much higher than the no growth environment of pre-industrial times.

- **Rise of Capitalism**: The era saw the consolidation of capitalism as the dominant economic system, with increased investments in factories and infrastructure

	1800	1850	Impact of industrialisation
Number of handloom weavers	160,000	40,000	-75%
Wages for handloom weavers	15 – 20 shillings	6 – 8 shillings	-60%
Number of workers in textile industry	240,000	331,000	+40%
Cotton production	52 million pounds	621 million pounds	+1,000%

The Second Industrial Revolution: from horse carts to building a car in 90 minutes

In 1878, people relied on gas lamps, oil lamps, kerosene, or candles to light their homes.

This is when Thomas Edison embarked on an ambitious project to create an incandescent light bulb that could be used by everyone.

At his Menlo Park, New Jersey, laboratory, he and his team experimented with thousands of different materials, testing various metals, plant fibres, and carbon-based substances.

In October 1879, they achieved a significant breakthrough by successfully testing a filament made from carbonised sewing thread in a vacuum, which lasted about 14.5 hours.

After testing over 6,000 different plant materials, Edison finally settled on carbonised bamboo in 1880. This new filament could last over 1,200 hours, making it suitable for widespread use and commercial production.

This was a major innovation. But a light bulb was useless without a way to deliver electricity to homes and businesses.

In 1882, Edison took the next bold step by opening the world's first power station on Pearl Street in New York City. On a September evening, as darkness fell over Manhattan, Edison flipped the switch, and for the first time, buildings across the city were illuminated by electric light. Crowds gathered on the streets, staring up in awe at the glowing windows...night had been conquered.

While Edison was enjoying the success of his direct current (DC) system, another inventor was working on a different approach — one that would have an even bigger impact on the future of electricity.

Nikola Tesla, an inventive mind from Serbia, had previously worked for Edison but left after a dispute over payment and a fundamental disagreement about the future of electricity. He was a proponent of alternating current (AC) and believed that it was a superior system to DC, but Edison dismissed the idea, famously remarking, "Fooling around with alternating current is just a waste of time."

Undeterred, Tesla found support in George Westinghouse, a prominent industrialist who recognised the potential in Tesla's ideas. Together, they entered into a rivalry with Edison, a conflict that became known as the "war of currents."

In his determination to defend his DC system, Edison even resorted to public demonstrations of AC's dangers, such as electrocuting animals, in an attempt to sway public opinion.

However, Tesla's AC system proved its value in 1895 when the first large-scale AC power plant was built at Niagara Falls. The power generated by the falls was transmitted over miles to light up Buffalo, New York.

When the switch was flipped, Tesla stood by the falls, quietly acknowledging the significance of the moment. "It is not a dream," he whispered to himself. "It is a simple feat of scientific electrical engineering."

Edison and Tesla, through their rivalry and inventions, ignited the Second Industrial Revolution. Factories no longer had to rely on daylight or steam engines — they could operate around the clock, fuelling unprecedented industrial growth. Homes were illuminated, cities connected, and the world began to hum with the power of electricity.

As electricity spread, its impact transformed nearly every aspect of daily life. Steel, made cheaply through the Bessemer process, became the foundation of the world's expanding infrastructure, from towering skyscrapers to extensive railways that linked distant cities. The chemical industry, driven by breakthroughs in synthetic production, brought innovations such as fertilisers that boosted agricultural yields and pharmaceuticals that improved health and longevity.

Meanwhile, the rise of the petroleum industry revolutionised transportation. Crude oil was refined into petrol, powering the first automobiles and laying the groundwork for a future where personal and commercial vehicles became essential to daily life. Henry Ford invented the moving assembly line at his Highland Park in Michigan and managed to manufacture a car in 90 minutes.

This made cars affordable for the masses, transforming how people travelled and even how cities were designed.

The world of communication also evolved rapidly. The invention of the telephone and the expansion of telegraph networks made it possible to connect with someone on the other side of the world in an instant — something we now take for granted with our smartphones. Electric trams and underground railways began to transform urban life, making cities more accessible and shaping modern public transportation systems.

The mass production of consumer goods became commonplace, leading to the rise of department stores and a culture of consumerism that persists to this day. From the light bulb that illuminates our homes to the cars we drive, the roads we travel, and the dishwasher in our kitchens, the technologies that emerged from this period laid the groundwork for the conveniences we consider essential in our everyday lives.

Impact on jobs: from craftsmen to factory workers

This technological revolution brought profound changes in employment and the nature of jobs.

One of the most significant shifts was the decline of middle-skilled jobs, particularly among craftsmen and operatives. In 1850, these workers made up nearly the entire manufacturing workforce, but by 1940, their share had dropped to around 50% as automated machinery reduced the need for highly skilled manual labour.

In place of these middle-skilled jobs, there was a marked increase in both unskilled labour and high-skilled corporate roles. Unskilled workers, who could operate the new machinery with minimal training, came to dominate nearly half of the manufacturing workforce by 1940. At the same time, the rise of complex industrial operations created demand for high-skilled positions, such as managers and engineers, who by 1940 made up about 10% of the workforce.

This shift also led to significant occupational switching, particularly among different age groups. Younger workers were more adaptable, often moving into emerging high-skilled roles, while older workers, displaced by technology, were more likely to shift into lower-skilled or unskilled positions, often facing downward mobility. Sectoral transformations also reshaped the labour market, with manufacturing employment growing sharply while agricultural jobs declined due to advancements in farming technology.

Polarisation, strikes, and the rise of labour movements

The second industrial revolution was not without its challenges. While the rise of factories and mass production created millions of new jobs, it also led to **wage polarisation**. High-skilled workers, such as engineers and managers, benefited from higher wages, while unskilled factory workers often faced long hours, low pay, and dangerous working conditions.

This growing inequality led to labour unrest. Workers, especially those in low-paying, unskilled jobs, began to organise and protest the harsh conditions. Strikes became a common form of resistance, as workers demanded better wages, safer working environments, and shorter hours. The rise of labour unions, like the American Federation of Labor (AFL), gave workers a platform to fight for their rights, pushing back against the concentration of wealth and power in the hands of industrialists.

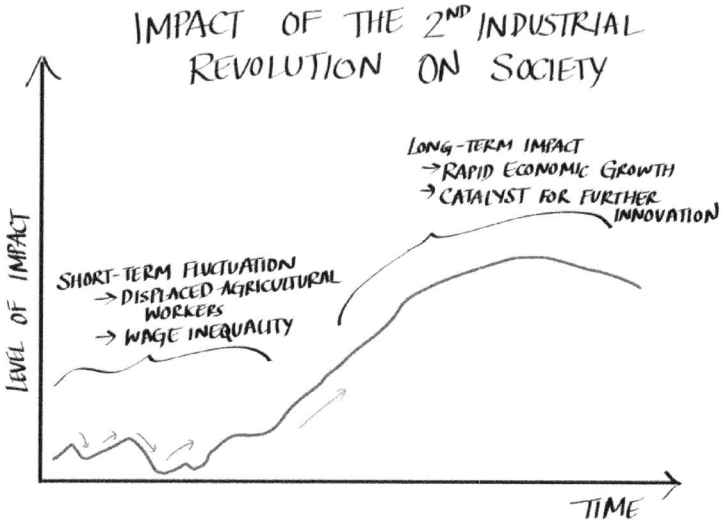

IMPACT OF THE 2ᴺᴰ INDUSTRIAL REVOLUTION ON SOCIETY

LONG-TERM IMPACT
→ RAPID ECONOMIC GROWTH
→ CATALYST FOR FURTHER INNOVATION

SHORT-TERM FLUCTUATION
→ DISPLACED AGRICULTURAL WORKERS
→ WAGE INEQUALITY

LEVEL OF IMPACT

TIME

The period also saw the rise of socialist movements that advocated for the rights of workers and critiqued the capitalist systems that profited from industrialisation while leaving many workers behind. These movements laid the groundwork for later reforms that would improve working conditions and labour rights in the 20th century.

Will AI change our lives like electricity?

Can we draw similar parallels between AI and the Second Industrial Revolution? Just as electricity and mass production transformed life in the late 19th and early 20th centuries, today's AI technologies could change industries, workplaces, and even daily routines in ways we're only beginning to imagine. The Second Industrial Revolution brought a wave of new products, from household appliances to automobiles, that **lifted standards of living, created jobs, and redefined the modern lifestyle**. However, alongside these advancements, **polarisation** emerged as some workers found themselves at risk of being left behind by the speed of change.

But those who thrived were often skilled managers and engineers, while many who worked on the factory floor faced low wages and demanding conditions. Workers came together to secure better protections, leading to reforms that would eventually shape modern labour standards.

The question now is: will AI bring similar benefits — and challenges? AI promises to open new industries, boost productivity, and offer economic growth, but could it also deepen divides between high-skilled and lower-skilled roles? Will it give rise to new social movements as workers seek a share in its benefits? Or will it instead drive a future where both growth and prosperity are more broadly shared?

As we look ahead, these questions remain. With thoughtful policies and inclusive planning, there's a path for AI to build on the positive legacy of past revolutions, lifting standards of living while addressing the social impacts that come with major change.

Summary of the Second Industrial Revolution

Description: Occurred from the late 19th century into the early 20th century, characterised by the expansion and invention of industries like steel, electricity, automotive and chemicals, and the rise of mass production techniques.

Main Impact on Employment:

- **Expansion of factory work**: Employment in manufacturing industries grew rapidly, with millions of new jobs created in sectors like automotive, electrical goods, and chemicals.
- **Semi-skilled labour demand**: The rise of assembly lines and mass production required a large workforce of semi-skilled workers. In the U.S., the number of factory workers doubled between 1880 and 1920.

Those Who Benefited:

- **Engineers and managers**: As industries grew more complex, the demand for managerial and engineering expertise increased, leading to higher wages and job security for these workers.
- **Industrial workers in new sectors**: Workers in rapidly growing industries like automobiles and electrical goods enjoyed relatively stable employment and improved wages compared to previous generations.

Those Who Were Left Behind:

- **Craftsmen and Artisans**: Mass production techniques, like assembly lines, further eroded the value of skilled craftsmanship. Jobs in new industries often required fewer specialised skills, leaving artisans with limited opportunities.
- **Agricultural Workers**: Improved mechanisation, including steam and gas-powered machinery, continued to decrease farm labour needs, accelerating migration from rural areas to urban factories.

Impact on Society:

- **Social Stratification**: The wealth generated by industrialists led to the rise of a wealthy capitalist class, while working-class families often lived in poor conditions. This period also saw the rise of labour unions as workers organised to fight for better wages and conditions.
- **Urbanisation and Public Health**: Rapid urbanisation continued, leading to overcrowded cities, but also to the development of public health initiatives and infrastructure, such as sewer systems and public hospitals.

Impact on Economy:

- **Economic Expansion**: This period saw rapid economic growth, with the U.S. economy growing by an average of 4% annually between 1870 and 1913. Global trade expanded, and the emergence of large corporations transformed the business landscape.
- **Technological Innovation**: The period was marked by a surge in technological innovation, leading to productivity gains across multiple sectors, particularly in steel production and electricity.

Metric	1880	1930	Impact of Industrialisation
Number of workers in agriculture (U.S.)	~7 million	~10 million	+40%
Agricultural output (U.S.)	~2.5 billion bushels (corn)	~3.6 billion bushels (corn)	+44%
Number of workers in steel industry (U.S.)	~100,000	~500,000	+400%

Metric	1880	1930	Impact of Industrialisation
Steel output (U.S.)	~1.25 million tons	~56 million tons	+4,380%
Number of workers in automotive industry (U.S.)	~5,000	~400,000	+7,900%
Automobile output (U.S.)	~2,000 units	~4.5 million units	+224,900%

The Third industrial revolution: it started with a mouse?

In December 1968, Douglas Engelbart stood on a stage in San Francisco, prepared to present a vision that had driven his work for nearly two decades. His journey to this moment was marked by persistence and a belief in the potential of technology to transform how people interact with information.

Born in 1925 on a small farm near Portland, Oregon, Engelbart grew up during the Great Depression, a time when life required hard work and resourcefulness. His interest in technology began during World War II, when he served as a radar technician in the U.S. Navy, sparking a fascination with electronic displays and their potential beyond military use.

After the war, Engelbart returned to Oregon State University to complete his degree in electrical engineering. In 1951, he had what he described as a "big dream" moment that led him to reconsider his future. He imagined a world where computers could be used not just for calculations, but as tools to enhance human intelligence and tackle complex problems — a concept that was unconventional at a time when computers were used for basic number-crunching tasks.

Engelbart encountered considerable scepticism. Early efforts to gain support for his ideas were met with resistance, as many experts saw his vision of interactive computing as impractical. Nonetheless, Engelbart remained committed to his goal. He left a secure job at NACA (the precursor to NASA) to pursue his research, eventually establishing his work at the Stanford Research Institute (SRI) in Menlo Park, California.

At SRI, Engelbart built a team and secured funding from the Department of Defense's ARPA, which enabled him to develop pioneering technologies. By 1968, Engelbart and his team had created the oNLine System (NLS), which included early versions of technologies now commonplace: the

49

computer mouse, graphical user interfaces, hypertext links, and real-time collaborative computing (think Google Docs).

On 9 December 1968, Engelbart showcased these innovations at the Fall Joint Computer Conference in San Francisco in a presentation titled "A research centre for augmenting human intellect." Known today as **"the mother of all demos,"** this 90-minute presentation introduced the audience to new possibilities in computing. Engelbart demonstrated how users could interact with text on a screen, edit documents in real-time, and navigate using what would later become known as the computer mouse.

Engelbart's work, once considered far-fetched, was now recognised as forward-thinking. This event marked a key moment in the development of the Digital Revolution. But this was only the beginning. The technologies Engelbart introduced contributed significantly to the evolution of computing: the mouse, the graphical user interface (GUI), hyperlinks, word processing, and even video conferencing.

New industries were created

The Digital Revolution, which began in the 1960s and extended into the early 21st century, marked the Third Industrial Revolution. It was defined by the rise of digital technologies, including computers, the Internet, and automation, and it fundamentally altered the job market.

High-skilled jobs grew significantly, particularly in fields like software development, IT management, and digital marketing. These roles emerged as computing and the Internet became more prevalent, creating demand for a workforce adept at leveraging new technologies.

At the same time, low-skilled service jobs in sectors like retail, hospitality, and personal care grew, as these roles were less susceptible to automation than middle-skilled jobs. However, the middle of the labour market — particularly routine cognitive jobs like clerical work or assembly line tasks

— suffered heavy losses. For example, clerical jobs in the U.S. declined by **30%** between 1980 and 2000 as office tasks became increasingly digitised and automated.

The rise of digital technologies created entirely new industries. IT and software development became one of the fastest-growing sectors, with software development employment increasing by over 150% between 1990 and 2010. The "app economy" generated billions of dollars and millions of jobs globally by the mid-2010s.

Digital workers did well, others less so

The shift towards digitalisation led to good prospects for those in **highly digital jobs,** who earned significantly more than those in medium- or low-digital occupations. By 2016, workers in highly digital jobs earned an average of **$72,896**, compared to **$48,274** for medium-digital jobs and **$30,393** for low-digital jobs.

This wage divide underscores the growing income inequality driven by digitalisation, where those with high-tech skills thrived while low- and middle-skilled workers often faced stagnating or declining wages.

The changing landscape of work was also evident in the digital skills required for different jobs. In 2002, 56% of jobs required low levels of digital skills, 40% required medium digital skills, and just 5% required high digital skills. By 2016, the job market had shifted significantly: 23% of jobs required high digital skills, 48% required medium digital skills, and the share of jobs needing low digital skills had dropped to 30%.

This shift not only transformed the nature of work but also highlighted the widening gap between those who could adapt to new digital technologies and those left behind.

The spread of digital technologies further exposed job automation risks. Around 60% of tasks in low-digital jobs, like retail or manual labour, were susceptible to automation, while only 30% of tasks in high-digital jobs faced similar risks. This further widened the gap between workers who adapted to digital tools and those whose jobs were vulnerable to technological displacement.

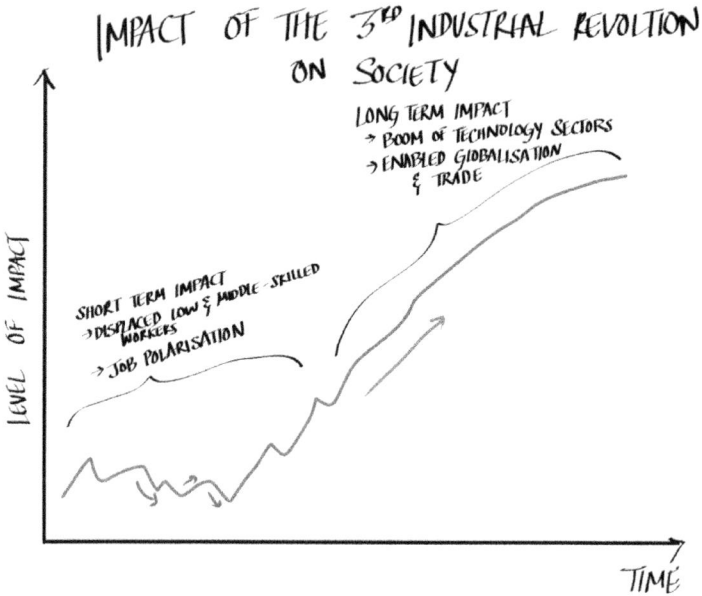

IMPACT OF THE 3ᴿᴰ INDUSTRIAL REVOLUTION ON SOCIETY

LONG TERM IMPACT
→ BOOM OF TECHNOLOGY SECTORS
→ ENABLED GLOBALISATION & TRADE

SHORT TERM IMPACT
→ DISPLACED LOW & MIDDLE-SKILLED WORKERS
→ JOB POLARISATION

LEVEL OF IMPACT

TIME

Will AI bring similar disruption?

Much like the Third Industrial Revolution, today's AI revolution raises important questions about the future of jobs and wages. Will we see a similar polarisation, where workers in AI-related jobs thrive while others are left behind?

In the same way **digitalisation created new high-paying jobs but left many others struggling**, AI may do the same. Those with the skills to leverage AI will likely see wage growth and job security, while many lower-skilled or routine jobs may be automated. Just as digital skills became a prerequisite for economic success, it's likely that AI literacy will be essential for the workforce of the future.

As we continue to navigate the Fourth Industrial Revolution, will AI bring new opportunities for workers across the board? Or will it further entrench wage inequality and displace workers unable to adapt? The challenges of job displacement, polarisation, and automation may once again force society to rethink how to ensure inclusive economic growth in a rapidly changing world.

Summary of the Third Industrial Revolution

Name: Third Industrial Revolution (Digital Revolution)

Description: Beginning in the mid-20th century, this revolution was driven by the transition from analogue and mechanical devices to digital technologies, including computers, the Internet, and automated production systems.

Main Impact on Employment:

- **Job Polarisation**: Growth in high-skilled jobs in technology, finance, and professional services, alongside an increase in low-skilled service jobs. Middle-skilled jobs, particularly those involving routine tasks, declined due to automation.
- **Automation**: The adoption of computers and digital technologies led to significant automation of manufacturing and clerical tasks, displacing many middle-skilled workers. For example, from 1980 to 2010, the share of U.S. manufacturing jobs fell from around 22% to 10%.

Those Who Benefited:

- **High-skilled workers in technology sectors**: Those with skills in software development, IT, and related fields saw significant wage growth and job opportunities.
- **Entrepreneurs in digital industries**: The rise of the Internet and digital platforms created new business opportunities, leading to the rapid growth of companies like Microsoft, Apple, and Amazon.

Those Who Were Left Behind:

- **Middle-skilled workers**: Particularly those in manufacturing and clerical jobs, faced job losses due to automation and offshoring. For example, wages for middle-skilled U.S. workers stagnated, growing only 12% in real terms from 1973 to 2013, despite productivity gains.

- **Low-skilled workers**: While some found employment in service sectors, these jobs often paid less and offered less job security compared to the manufacturing jobs they replaced.

Impact on Society:

- **Income Inequality**: The Gini coefficient in the U.S. rose from around 0.35 in the 1970s to 0.49 by 2019, reflecting increasing income inequality. The benefits of technological advancements were disproportionately captured by those at the top of the income distribution.
- **Changes in Work Culture**: The rise of the gig economy and flexible work arrangements led to changes in job stability and benefits, with more workers facing precarious employment conditions.

Impact on Economy:

- **Economic Growth**: The global economy expanded significantly, driven by the rise of the digital economy. The IT sector became a major contributor to GDP in many advanced economies. For example, in the U.S., the tech industry accounted for 10% of GDP by 2019.
- **Globalisation**: The Digital Revolution facilitated the globalisation of trade and services, enabling companies to operate across borders more efficiently. However, this also contributed to the offshoring of jobs and increased competition in labour markets worldwide.

Metric	1970	2020	Impact of Digital Revolution
Number of workers in manufacturing (U.S.)	~19 million	~12 million	-37%
Manufacturing output (U.S.)	~ $1.2 trillion (inflation-adjusted)	~ $2.3 trillion	+92%
Number of workers in IT/Tech industry (U.S.)	~400,000	~12 million	+2,567%
IT/Technology industry output (U.S.)	~ $50 billion (inflation-adjusted)	~ $1.9 trillion	+3,700%
Number of workers in retail (U.S.)	~7 million	~15 million	+114%
E-commerce sales (U.S.)	~ $0 (negligible)	~ $800 billion	Explosive Growth
Number of workers in e-commerce (U.S.)	Negligible	~1.2 million	Significant Growth

How the technological revolutions impacted jobs and the economy

When we consider the impacts of the three Industrial Revolutions on jobs and the economy, **the overall trend in quality of life and work has been positive.** Our standard of living is higher compared to the 18th century. The average person enjoys improved health, access to education, and amenities that would have seemed unimaginable in earlier times.

In terms of employment, the shift from manual, physically demanding jobs to more skilled roles generally improved working conditions and safety, even though these benefits weren't universally felt at the time.

Below, we'll examine the figures to see in more detail how each industrial revolution impacted the economy and jobs. This data will reveal the trends in GDP growth, unemployment, and the types of roles that emerged or transformed in response to each wave of innovation.

Impact on Employment

When we look at unemployment rates in the UK — the country that experienced all three industrial revolutions — it's striking to see that these technological transformations didn't have a noticeable impact on overall unemployment. Instead, the major fluctuations in employment over the past two centuries were due to macroeconomic shocks, such as the First World War, the 1929 Great Depression, and the recession of the 1980s. These events caused clear spikes in unemployment, whereas the waves of industrial change brought on by new technologies did not.

In other words, **from a macroeconomic standpoint, the industrial revolutions didn't significantly impact employment rates, either positively or negatively.** Although new jobs emerged and others disappeared as industries evolved, the shifts in employability appear to have been gradual enough that they didn't disrupt the broader employment landscape.

This suggests that, while industrial revolutions transformed the **nature of work** and spurred economic growth, their effect on overall unemployment remained relatively steady in the long term.

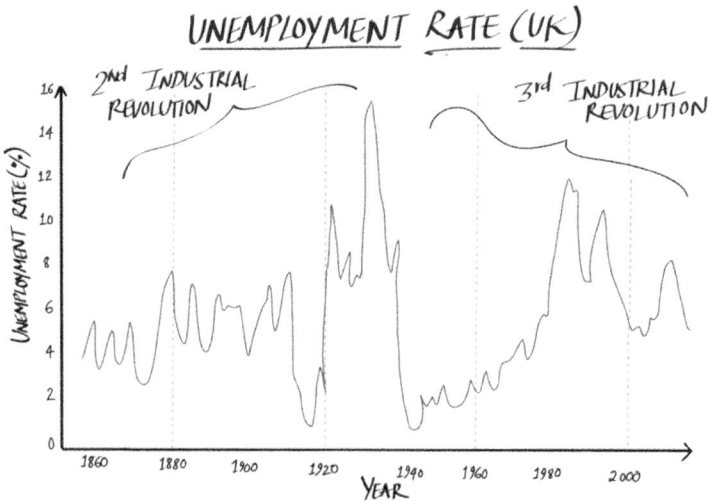

UNEMPLOYMENT RATE (UK)

The **First Industrial Revolution** saw a shift from agrarian economies to industrial ones, as mechanised factories replaced traditional craft-based work. Although skilled artisans, like the Luddites, were displaced by machines, society as a whole adapted as new factory-based jobs emerged.

In the **Second Industrial Revolution**, the rise of mass production systems and the spread of electricity transformed industries once again. This period saw the workforce polarise between low-skilled factory workers and a growing class of high-skilled managers and engineers. Despite this, unemployment was shaped more by broader economic conditions than by technological advancements alone.

During the **Third Industrial Revolution**, marked by digitalisation and the rise of automation, the job market experienced a hollowing out of middle-skilled roles, such as clerical work. Computers and software began automating routine tasks, leading to significant declines in these sectors. However, new industries — like software development and digital marketing — expanded, providing opportunities for high-skilled workers.

Impact on Wages and Inequality

During the Industrial Revolutions, different sectors and jobs did very well, whereas others did not. **This led to increased inequality,** as measured by the Gini Index of global inequality. In 1820, global income inequality was at a lower level with a Gini Index of 0.60, but by 1910 — following the First and Second Industrial Revolutions — it peaked at 0.72.

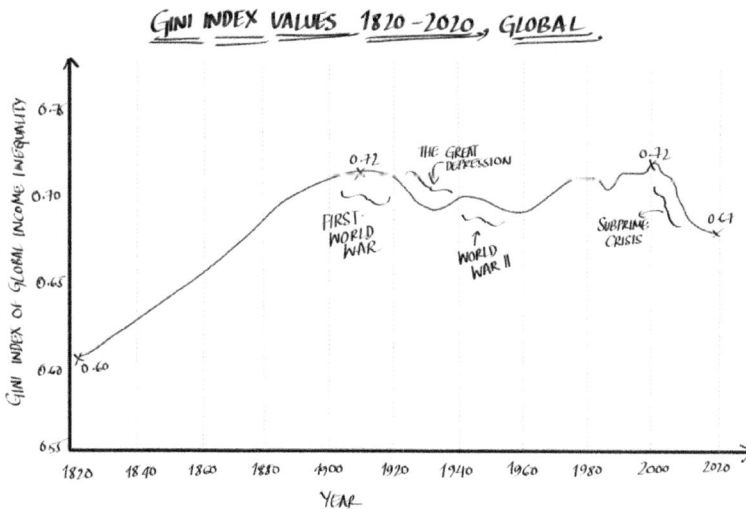

GINI INDEX VALUES 1870-2020, GLOBAL

The pattern continued through the 20th century, with each economic and technological revolution widening the gap. Although economic shocks like the Great Depression and

World War II temporarily disrupted this trend, inequality climbed again during periods of rapid technological advancement, as seen in the post-war years and particularly during the Third Industrial Revolution.

In the Third Industrial Revolution and the digital economy, wage disparity between high- and low-paid workers became especially pronounced. Workers equipped with digital skills saw their earnings soar, while those left behind by automation faced stagnant or declining incomes.

By 2016, for example, workers in highly digital jobs earned an average of $72,896, compared to just $30,393 for those in low-digital roles. This **wage polarisation** contributed to the ongoing increase in income inequality, as middle-skilled jobs were increasingly automated, forcing displaced workers into lower-paying positions in less digitised sectors.

The shift towards a digital economy not only altered the types of jobs available but also transformed the skills necessary for success. In 2002, over half of all jobs required only low levels of digital skills, but by 2016, that figure had fallen to 30%. Conversely, the demand for high digital skills rose from 5% to 23% over the same period, highlighting how quickly digitalisation has reshaped the labour market and exacerbated income disparities.

Impact on Economic Growth

Each of the three industrial revolutions contributed to significant economic growth, reflected in steady increases in GDP per capita. The First Industrial Revolution led to sustained economic development through the mechanisation of production, helping to create new industries and jobs.

In the Second Industrial Revolution, widespread adoption of new technologies like electricity and mass production triggered a sharp rise in productivity and living standards.

The Third Industrial Revolution continued this trend, with advancements in digital technologies and automation driving productivity gains and boosting economic output. However, the benefits were not uniformly distributed across all sectors, as some industries thrived while others were left behind.

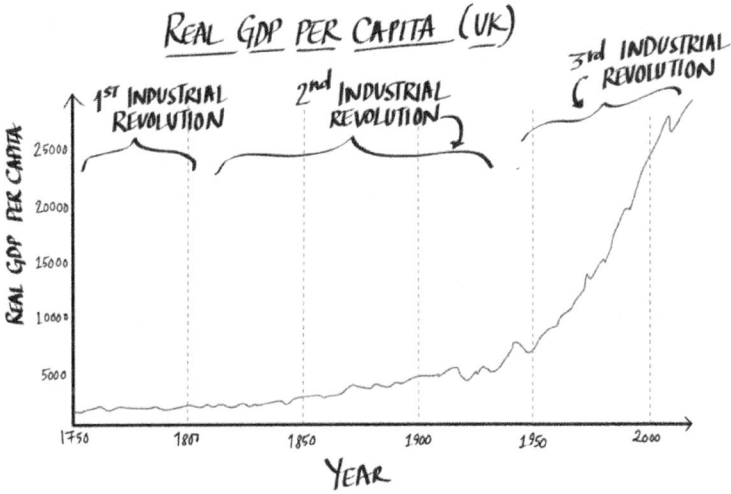

REAL GDP PER CAPITA (UK)

Conclusion

While each industrial revolution brought long-term economic growth, their effects on employment and wage distribution were more complex. Unemployment trends were driven by broader macroeconomic factors, such as recessions and global trade shifts, rather than by technological disruptions alone. However, the revolutions did lead to job polarisation, as high-skilled workers benefited the most from the new technologies, while many middle and low-skilled workers faced stagnating wages.

Will AI follow the same patterns?

Looking ahead to the **Fourth Industrial Revolution**, driven by **AI and machine learning**, the lessons from history offer a useful perspective. Will we once again see a segment of the workforce, like the Luddites, struggle to adapt as society overall grows more prosperous? The **First Industrial Revolution** showed that some workers may fall behind, but economies tend to generate new opportunities over time. Will AI lead to similar adaptation?

The **Second Industrial Revolution** illustrated the risk of **job polarisation**, where a growing divide emerged between low-paid workers and highly skilled managers and engineers. Could AI exacerbate this divide, creating a new class of highly paid AI specialists while further pushing lower-skilled workers into precarious employment? History also shows that times of economic transformation have often led to **labour movements** aimed at defending workers' rights. Could we see the rise of similar movements in response to AI-driven automation?

Finally, the **Third Industrial Revolution** created entirely new industries and a class of highly paid digital workers, while other sectors saw wage stagnation and job loss.

Will AI create a similar dynamic, where those who master AI technologies reap the rewards while others are left behind?

Overall, each of the previous industrial revolutions ultimately led to greater **wealth and prosperity** for society as a whole. The question now is whether AI will follow the same path, creating broad economic gains and improving standards of living. Will the **Fourth Industrial Revolution** follow the same pattern as its three predecessors. Or will it be different this time?

Let's discover the answer in the next chapter.

Part II:

We've Seen It Before, or This Time It's Different?

Exploring whether AI follows historical patterns or is a unique disruptor

"History doesn't repeat itself, but it often rhymes"

Mark Twain

"The four most dangerous words in investing are: this time it's different"

John Templeton

As a lover of history and a former practitioner in financial markets, I know it's tempting to think that things will unfold in ways we've never seen before — and more often than not, we end up being wrong.

The first three Industrial Revolutions offer strong support for those who side with Twain or Templeton — those who argue that AI is simply another technological shift, much like those we've seen before. Let's call this the **"We've Seen It Before"** camp. When it comes to jobs, this camp believes that while new technologies can disrupt certain groups — like the Luddites — they ultimately lead to job creation and benefit society as a whole.

However, there's another perspective: **"This Time It's Different"**. This camp doesn't dismiss history but contends that AI cannot be compared to the steam engine or electricity. In their view, AI will lead to a fundamentally different outcome, with the potential for widespread job losses and significant consequences for the future of work.

Are you in the WSIB or TTID camp?

It's a difficult question, and even experts can't agree. Take, for example, Yoshua Bengio, Geoffrey Hinton, and Yann LeCun — three of the world's most renowned specialists in Artificial Intelligence. In 2018, they were jointly awarded

66

the Turing Award for their groundbreaking work in deep learning. Often referred to as the "Godfathers of Deep Learning," the trio share decades of collaboration and success. They've known each other for more than 30 years, with Bengio meeting LeCun during his Master's studies and LeCun completing his postdoc under Hinton. Their careers have flourished in both academia and industry, with Hinton at Google, LeCun at Facebook/Meta, and Bengio as a leading AI entrepreneur.

But despite their shared history, their opinions on AI's future have diverged. In May 2023, Geoffrey Hinton resigned from Google, raising alarms about AI's rapid advancement and potential existential risks. At the same time, Bengio expressed concerns over the pace of AI development and the lack of safeguards. He admitted regretting his focus on innovation over safety.

In October 2024, Hinton, along with John Hopfield from Princeton, was awarded the Nobel Prize in Physics for his work on neural networks. In his Nobel interview, Hinton cautioned, "We're at a bifurcation point in history where, in the next few years, we need to figure out if we can control the existential threat AI might pose."

On the other hand, Yann LeCun remains optimistic. He argues that AI is far from being an existential risk, famously claiming that today's AI is still "dumber than cats." While acknowledging the potential for disruption, LeCun believes that AI will ultimately enhance productivity and create new jobs — just as past technological shifts have done.

Andrew Ng and Bill Gates similarly lean toward the WSIB perspective. Ng likens AI to a tool that enhances productivity, akin to electricity, rather than a threat to human employment. He contends that AI can be an equalising force, opening opportunities across sectors and helping workers become more efficient.

Bill Gates, too, is largely optimistic, seeing AI as a catalyst for productivity that will free workers to focus on higher-value, human-centric roles, especially in fields like healthcare and education. Both see AI as a transformative technology that will ultimately benefit society, even as it requires a rethinking of workforce skills.

Elon Musk, however, aligns squarely with the TTID camp. Musk has frequently voiced concerns that AI could evolve to pose an existential risk, not only in terms of job displacement but potentially even to humanity itself. His advocacy for strong regulatory oversight and caution reflects a deep-seated belief that AI has the potential to disrupt society in ways that previous technologies did not — and that it should not be left unchecked.

This division reflects the broader uncertainty surrounding AI's impact on employment and society. If the most prominent minds in the field cannot agree on whether AI's development will follow familiar patterns or bring unprecedented upheaval, then how can we approach decisions about the millions of jobs potentially affected?

To answer this question, we need a better understanding of the mechanism by which AI affects jobs.

Benefits of identifying a transmission mechanism

In economics, transmission mechanisms explain how a change in one part of a system affects other parts. For example, when a central bank cuts interest rates, lending becomes cheaper, businesses borrow more, invest, hire more workers, and employment increases. This chain of reactions can be analysed, tested, and refined.

Understanding this sequence is crucial for predicting technological impacts. It helps us break down simple assumptions — such as, "AI will eliminate jobs" — into a more nuanced view of how technological shifts actually ripple through industries and affect employment.

A similar transmission mechanism for AI ?

Let's explore the transmission mechanism between past technological revolutions and jobs to understand whether AI will follow a similar path, or if this time really is different.

In the Third Industrial Revolution, the Internet disrupted traditional industries like newspapers, forcing many journalists out of work. But at the same time, it created new fields such as digital marketing and online content creation, allowing workers to transition into new roles. This is an example of how disruption can displace jobs in one sector while creating opportunities in another.

The key question for AI is whether it will follow this same displacement-and-replacement cycle, or if its ability to replicate human cognitive tasks represents a more direct threat to jobs across all sectors.

The Internet Disrupted Newspapers: Journalists Found New Roles

Let's revisit the Third Industrial Revolution and the advent of computers, which ultimately led to the Internet. Overall, it created new jobs — 40% of today's jobs didn't exist 50 years ago. An industry that was significantly challenged by this shift was traditional media.

If you lived through the Internet revolution, you might remember **Red Herring**, the magazine that thrived by covering the explosive growth of the technology industry in the early 2000s. At its peak, it generated $100 million in revenue and employed 350 journalists.

Peter Rojas was one of them. He joined **Red Herring** in 1999, and in his own words, "during the dotcom boom, a 24-year-old with almost no journalism experience could wind up as associate editor of the fastest-growing magazine in America."

However, the bursting of the dot-com bubble rapidly put an end to Red Herring and Peter's dream job. The company went through multiple rounds of layoffs, and Peter was let go in 2001. By 2003, Red Herring went out of business.

As a broke writer, Peter decided to move from San Francisco to New York. With his skills as a technology writer but no jobs for journalists, he started a tech blog — **Gizmodo**.

Gizmodo was one of the first tech blogs focused on gadgets, consumer electronics, and technology news. Peter's fast-paced, concise posts on the latest gadgets appealed to a growing tech-savvy audience. Within a few years, Gizmodo became a major player in the tech media space, attracting millions of monthly visitors.

In 2004, Peter left **Gizmodo** to launch another tech blog — **Engadget** — which also grew into a major media site. Today, both Gizmodo and Engadget continue to attract millions of viewers each month.

The story of Peter Rojas and Red Herring offers an accelerated glimpse into the impact of the Internet on newspapers and journalists. The Internet moved readers away from newspapers and gave them more options in the form of blogs, social media, and videos. This led to falling readership, shrinking advertising revenue, and intense pressure on the industry.

In the United States, newspaper ad revenues fell by two-thirds, from $50 billion in 2005 to $15 billion in 2018.

Journalists were equally affected. Between 2008 and 2020, newsroom jobs in the U.S. dropped by 26%, with more than 30,000 journalists losing their positions.

What happened to journalists? Many, like Peter, leveraged their skills to transition into new careers. They moved into marketing, public relations, or content creation — fields that require strong writing, research, and storytelling abilities — skills they developed as journalists. Others moved into digital marketing, a new field that valued their expertise in creating engaging narratives and compelling copy.

The Internet disrupted newspapers, and journalists adapted by transitioning to new jobs. This is the core argument of the **"We've Seen It Before" (WSIB)** camp: while some jobs are lost, others are created in emerging industries.

Understanding the Transmission Mechanism for the Internet

But what was the transmission mechanism that led from the Internet's impact on newspapers to the job losses of tens of thousands of journalists, and ultimately, to their transition into other roles?

Let's follow the journey of Laura, a hypothetical journalist who works at **News Media**, a fictional news magazine. She loses her job and finds another position as a digital marketer at **Future Agency**.

- Laura is employed as a journalist.
- Her employer is a magazine — News Media.
- The magazine is part of a wider industry — press.

The Internet put pressure on her industry — press. **News Media** saw declining revenues and had to cut costs. They implemented layoffs, and Laura lost her job.

The primary impact of the Internet was on the industry — it increased competition on newspapers and magazines. For

Laura, it was a **collateral impact** because she worked in a company that was part of an industry struggling with heightened competition.

Luckily for Laura, she had strong writing and narrative skills that helped her find another job at Future Agency.

- She finds a new job — content marketer.
- Her new employer is a digital agency — Future Agency.
- The agency is part of a wider industry — digital marketing.

Here, the primary impact of the Internet was also on the industry, with a new sector — digital marketing — being created and now worth hundreds of billions of dollars. For Laura, it was a **collateral impact** where the Internet created new opportunities for jobs, and she could leverage her skills to get these jobs.

In other cases, journalists did not move into new industries, but were still able to find new opportunities because their skills were transferable to many other job roles in PR, communication, or marketing.

Technological revolutions had a collateral impact on jobs

Looking back at the previous technological revolutions, technology initially impacted certain sectors or industries, that then led to a **collateral impact on jobs**. These changes in industry dynamics often led to job losses in certain sectors while creating new job opportunities elsewhere.

For example, the First Industrial Revolution led to the introduction of steam-powered railways. It revolutionised transportation but also reduced reliance on canals and roads. The primary impact was on the transportation industry, and the collateral impact was felt by canal workers and carriage drivers who lost their jobs. For instance, the 30 stagecoaches that travelled daily between Manchester and Liverpool became obsolete.

On the other hand, railways also created new employment opportunities, with tens of thousands of workers in construction and operation, and new jobs in engineering and station services.

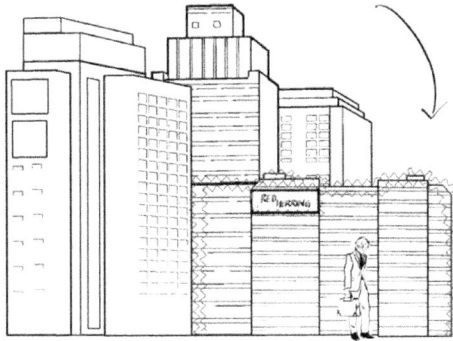

EXAMPLE OF COLLATERAL IMPACT:
TECHNOLOGY IMPACTS A COMPANY

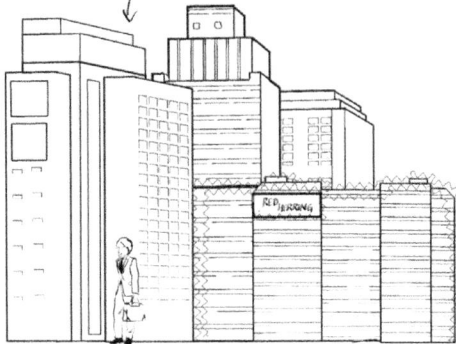

AFFECTED PEOPLE JUMP TO OTHER COMPANIES OR INDUSTRIES

During the Second Industrial Revolution, the transition from wooden ships to steel-hulled steamships caused significant shifts in the shipbuilding industry. In both the U.S. and Britain, the introduction of steam-powered steel ships led to a rapid decline in wooden shipbuilding. Thousands of jobs in wooden shipyards were lost as shipwrights and carpenters saw their roles diminish. For instance, shipyards along the U.S. Atlantic coast, which had specialised in wooden vessels, experienced steep declines after 1890.

At the same time, new jobs were created in steel shipbuilding and related industries. Britain's steel industry, particularly in cities like Sheffield, experienced a boom, with steel production for ships increasing significantly. By the 1880s, Britain was producing millions of tons of steel annually, and the demand for skilled labour in modern shipyards surged, creating tens of thousands of new jobs in the construction, engineering, and maintenance of steel-hulled ships.

The impact of new technologies on jobs can be seen as a natural outcome of innovation. New ways of doing things often lead to increased competition in some sectors, resulting in job losses, while other areas may see growth, with entirely new industries and job opportunities emerging.

In this sense, it's similar to the patterns we see in economic cycles or the typical evolution of a company.

In a growth cycle, industries and companies will need more manpower and hire more employees.

Or, a company could be subject to intense competition or make poor decisions, leading to layoffs.

In summary, technological revolutions primarily drive changes in processes, efficiency, and competitive dynamics within industries, rather than directly impacting jobs. The impact on jobs is collateral. The initial effect is on how things are done, which then leads to shifts in industry positions — some companies gain advantages while others face heightened competition. As a collateral result, these shifts trickle down to the workforce: some jobs are lost as certain industries decline, while others are created in sectors that thrive or emerge due to new technologies.

What Do Fashion Models, Translators, and Customer Service Agents Have in Common? AI Coming for Their Jobs…

Sam, Anne, and Lucy share a cosy flat in East London, managing to scrape by in the city's chaotic hustle. They've been close friends for years and have a great camaraderie, but lately, each has been feeling the weight of changes in their respective careers. With AI technologies becoming more capable and pervasive, they've started to notice shifts that feel too significant to ignore.

Sam: AI took his job as customer service agent

Sam works in customer service for a well-known UK retailer. His job has always been to answer customer queries, process orders, and troubleshoot issues for customers. But one Friday, he comes home looking defeated. His company has decided to replace the majority of its customer service agents with an AI chatbot system. The company calls it a move toward "greater efficiency," but Sam knows it's a cost-saving measure at his expense. He saw the changes coming as the number of calls dwindled, but he hadn't anticipated losing his job so soon. "I never thought I'd be replaced by a machine," he tells Anne and Lucy that evening. His friends try to comfort him, but Sam's worried. With limited skills beyond customer service, he wonders how he'll manage to find a new role that offers stability in a rapidly changing job market.

Anne: AI challenges translators

Anne, originally from France, moved to London after university. She's been working as a freelance translator, translating business documents and reports between French and English. But only a few weeks after Sam loses his job, Anne receives an email from one of her main clients — a multinational corporation that's now using AI translation tools instead of human translators.

This client was a major source of income, and Anne is shaken by the sudden change. Initially, she thinks it's a fluke. But soon, more clients follow suit, explaining that AI offers faster turnaround times and lower costs. Sitting with Sam over coffee one morning, Anne confesses her fears. "It's like I'm watching my career disappear," she says. She's used to the ebb and flow of freelance work, but AI translation tools have drastically altered the landscape, and she's unsure how to adapt.

Lucy: Will AI take over modelling?

Lucy, meanwhile, works as a model. She's built a decent portfolio over the years, modelling for fashion brands and high-street retailers. But as she watches her friends struggle, Lucy starts to feel a creeping sense of dread herself. Recently, she saw that Mango, a popular fashion brand, used AI-generated models in their new Sunset Dream collection for the Mango Teen youth line, which is now available in 95 markets.

The AI models were created to look flawless, and the brand didn't need photographers, makeup artists, or lighting technicians. Lucy mentions this to Anne and Sam one evening, confessing that she's worried the industry could move in that direction. "They say AI models are cheaper, faster, and never need a break," she says. While her agency has assured her that real models will always have a place in fashion, Lucy is afraid that modelling — already a short career — could be even shorter for her.

Some face uncertainty but others do very well

As the three friends sit in their flat, they reflect on how quickly AI is changing their lives, and not in ways they ever anticipated. The reality feels overwhelming, but what confuses them most is that their friend Max is thriving. Max finished his Master's in Biology just two years ago and landed a role at Google DeepMind right out of school. Now he's working on groundbreaking projects that blur the lines between biology and computing. "He's part of the team that developed AlphaFold," Lucy says, looking at the others with a mixture of admiration and disbelief. "They're doing things that could change medicine forever, and now his company's founders just won a Nobel Prize."

Lucy looks between them. "Maybe we should try to find ways to work with AI?" They fall into silence, each lost in their own tangled thoughts. Sure, it sounds reasonable, but how? For Sam, does it mean learning something completely new — coding, perhaps? For Anne, could she find some angle in translation that AI hasn't already taken over? Maybe there's a way to focus on the nuances that only a human can spot, but she wonders if clients would even pay extra for that. Lucy thinks about her own situation; is there really anything she can bring to modelling that an AI can't just replicate or even enhance? They all know Max is thriving, but he works at DeepMind. For them, it's different. What could they actually do that AI isn't already doing better, faster, and cheaper?

Is it different this time?

This story is fictional, but **it is not far from reality**. Customer service roles have already decreased by 16% on freelance platforms since the introduction of ChatGPT, and a third of translators have already lost jobs to AI. Brands like Mango and McDonald's have already begun using AI-generated models for their advertising campaigns.

Is it different this time? Is AI different from previous technologies?

AI has a direct impact on jobs

Let's break down the transmission mechanism for **Owl**, a translator working for the hypothetical language app LearnLanguage.

- Owl works in a specific job — in her case, translator.
- Her employer is a language learning app — LearnLanguage.
- Which is part of a broader industry — mobile applications.

Unlike previous industrial revolutions, where changes in industry or process had collateral impacts on jobs, **Owl's job loss is a direct impact of AI.** It's not as if AI-driven pressure caused mobile apps or platforms like LearnLanguage to force Owl out of her role. In fact, mobile apps are thriving, and companies like LearnLanguage are performing remarkably well.

Owl lost her job because, given the choice between her and an AI, LearnLanguage decided that AI was the more efficient option. It wasn't external pressure from competitors driving the change; rather, the company saw AI as a viable replacement for her specific role and went with it.

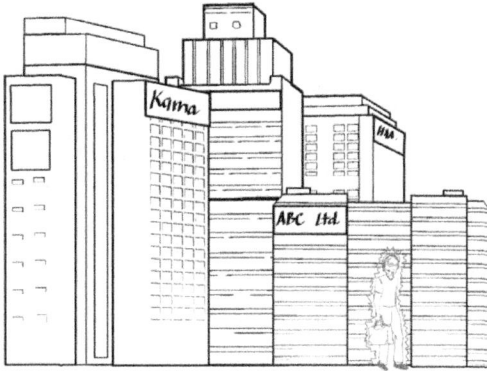

WHEN THE IMPACT IS DIRECT,
WHERE CAN YOU GO?

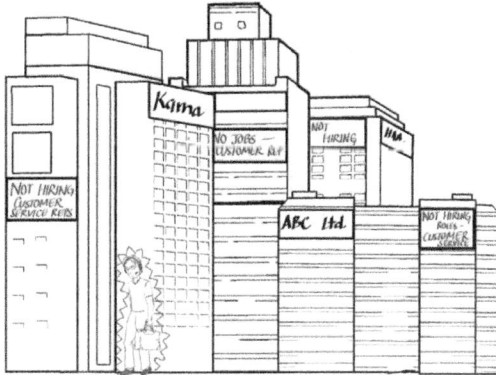

This is where we clearly see the difference between previous technologies such as the Internet and AI today. The Internet's impact on Laura was collateral. She lost her job as an indirect result of changes in her industry, and her new role was also a byproduct of how the Internet transformed her field.

81

By contrast, AI's impact on Owl is direct: her specific skills were targeted and replaced.

In previous technological revolutions, change began at the industry level — transforming sectors, companies, or processes — and only then did it affect people, either positively or negatively. With AI, the impact is different: it operates directly at the level of individual roles, transforming skills and tasks themselves. Rather than reshaping industries first, AI reaches straight to the people doing the work, bypassing the traditional industry-to-people pathway altogether.

Why does AI have a direct impact?

Historically, technological revolutions primarily influenced tools, processes, or ecosystems, leading to indirect or collateral changes in the job market. This meant that while specific roles were disrupted, new opportunities often emerged. However, the AI-fication of jobs is unique in that it directly replicates human skills, making its impact more immediate and personal.

Previous technological revolutions: tools, processes, and ecosystems

Throughout history, technology has enhanced human productivity by improving the tools, processes, and ecosystems in which people work. While these innovations sometimes led to job losses, they often created opportunities for displaced workers to transition into new roles that leveraged their existing skills.

For example, **tools** like the steam engine revolutionised transportation and manufacturing, allowing workers to shift from physically demanding jobs to operating machinery. Similarly, the introduction of computers enabled fields like accounting to move from manual, paper-based ledgers to digital spreadsheets, improving accuracy and efficiency.

Processes were also redefined. The assembly line made production faster and cheaper by breaking down tasks into simple, repetitive actions. While skilled craftsmen lost their roles, new positions for line workers and technicians emerged, still requiring human involvement.

Finally, **ecosystems** were reshaped. The Internet, for instance, restructured commerce and media, leading to the decline of traditional sectors like print journalism, but enabling the rise of digital marketing and e-commerce, creating new roles for displaced workers.

In these cases, technology **indirectly affected jobs** by enhancing productivity and creating opportunities for workers to apply their skills in new, emerging fields.

How AI differs: skills

The AI-fication of jobs directly impacts work because AI replicates human skills, particularly in cognitive tasks. Unlike past innovations that mainly improved tools and processes, AI can **perform tasks traditionally associated with human intelligence**. This marks a significant shift from indirect impacts to direct skill substitution.

Technologies like deep learning and natural language processing are not just about making tasks faster or more accurate — they perform tasks that once required human judgement. For example, models like GPT-4 can pass professional exams, often outperforming humans. AI can now generate creative content, analyse data, and even make strategic recommendations in real-time, often with greater precision than humans.

Tasks once thought to require a human touch — like writing, data analysis, and customer service — are now within AI's reach. Translation tools such as Google Translate or DeepL provide high-quality translations, reducing the need for human translators. AI-driven chatbots handle customer service queries quickly and efficiently. Even in creative fields, AI-generated models, music, and artwork are now commercially viable, posing a direct challenge to professionals in those areas.

This AI-fication of tasks doesn't just enhance productivity — it can replace human input. As AI systems improve, they move closer to performing tasks across a wide range of disciplines, posing significant risks for job displacement. AI doesn't just change how work is done — it raises questions about who will be doing the work in the future as machines increasingly take over tasks once thought to require human intelligence.

Why AI feels so personal

The reason the AI-fication of jobs feels more personal than past technological shifts is that AI blurs the line between what machines do and what humans uniquely offer. While past technologies made work faster or cheaper, AI directly competes with human skills, performing the very tasks that define many jobs.

This direct impact on human abilities creates a sense of vulnerability that wasn't present in previous technological shifts. Jobs are no longer lost because industries evolve — now, jobs are disappearing because AI is replacing the core skills that humans bring to work. AI's rapid deployment makes it feel like a competitor to human expertise, forcing workers to confront a fundamental question:

If AI can replicate human skills, what does that mean for the future of the workforce?

This is why the AI-fication of jobs feels different — it doesn't just enhance productivity, it challenges the very value of human expertise in an AI-driven world.

This Time It's Different. Really.

Is AI different from previous technological revolutions, or have we seen this pattern before? On the surface, it might seem like just another shift, much like the steam engine or the Internet. But if we ask ourselves honestly, did the Internet ever feel personally threatening? Did the rise of smartphones, virtual reality, or even earlier automation waves ever feel like they might replace us as individuals? Most likely not.

Perhaps your company was disrupted by these changes, or maybe you found new opportunities in a sector that emerged because of them. For most of us, though, these technologies didn't directly challenge our own roles — they shaped industries and created shifts that indirectly impacted us. With AI, however, it feels different. This time, the disruption hits closer to home. It's not just an industry-wide or company-level change; it's about AI replicating specific tasks we do every day.

The personal impact of AI is widespread, touching on both cognitive and creative jobs that once seemed uniquely human. Unlike the smartphone or Internet, AI feels intrusive because it questions the skills we depend on. The question we now face isn't about adapting to a new tool or process, but rather, "How is AI affecting me directly?"

A fundamental shift in the transmission mechanism

The reason AI feels so personal lies in its transmission mechanism — how it impacts jobs compared to past technologies. In previous revolutions, technology's effect was collateral: it transformed industries, then companies adapted, and eventually, this restructuring reached workers. This traditional "technology-to-industry-to-people" pathway made the changes feel more gradual and often gave workers time to adapt.

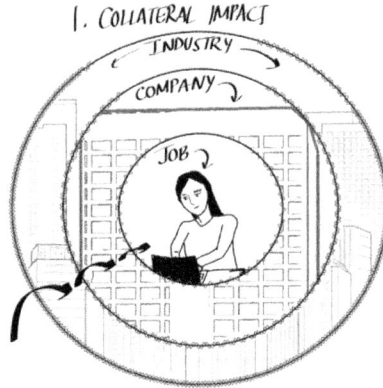

I. COLLATERAL IMPACT

With AI, this process changes entirely. AI can target specific human skills directly, bypassing the traditional sequence and going straight to the individual roles. It doesn't need an industry shift: its impact on people is immediate and more tangible.

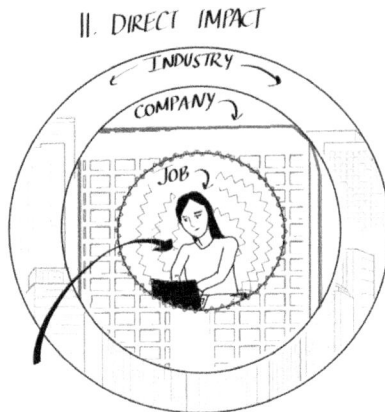

II. DIRECT IMPACT

This shift from collateral to direct impact is not only personal but also faster. When technology affects jobs directly, the change can be swift and more unpredictable. This simpler, faster transmission mechanism is what makes AI unique. It challenges us on a personal level, but also allows us to model and anticipate its effects in a new way. While the "This Time It's Different" camp is right in saying AI's impact is fundamentally unique, it's essential to remember that different doesn't have to mean negative.

Different doesn't necessarily mean Negative

It's important to stress that just because AI's impact on jobs is direct, **it doesn't mean we must assume a pessimistic outcome.** Our analysis has shown that this time it is different, but it has not concluded that the disruption will result in mass unemployment or a loss of all jobs as anticipated by the TTID camp.

A direct impact means **we should anticipate a different pattern from previous technological revolutions**, as well as a distinctive way in which job transformations will materialise. We cannot therefore rely solely on the experience of past technological shifts as a blueprint.

The directness of AI's effect on jobs also brings an advantage: it allows for a more straightforward modelling of outcomes, avoiding some of the complex, indirect mechanisms seen with prior technology shifts.

For a problem as complex as AI and jobs, this is a significant benefit, helping us to leverage existing frameworks to predict how AI will impact the workforce.

This is what we will do in the next chapter, where we will explore the CDE Innovation Prism, a model that has proven effective in analysing the impact of technology on many different sectors. This will provide a good conceptual foundation to think about AI and jobs.

Part III:

The CDE Innovation Prism: A Framework for Predicting the Future

Using a structured approach to model the future impact of technology

I've always wanted to be an entrepreneur, I don't know why or where it came from.

Coming from an Asian background, entrepreneurship wasn't something typically encouraged. In many families like mine, the focus was often on becoming a doctor or securing a stable job in a large company — seen as the best way to make the most of our education. Entrepreneurship was perceived as risky and unconventional.

I was lucky enough to study at MIT right in the middle of the Internet revolution — and what a time it was!

The campus was alive with innovation everywhere I looked. I remember the MIT $50K competition, where teams were pitching projects like Akamai, which went on to build the backbone of the Internet as we know it. In our labs, we were experimenting with emerging tech, like 3D printers, that felt futuristic at the time. Some of the students were walking around campus with early wearable tech: glasses connected to laptops they carried in their backpacks.

Meanwhile, across the country, two Stanford grads were developing PageRank, the algorithm that would become the foundation of Google. Being surrounded by breakthrough ideas in the early days of the Internet gave me first-hand insight into how transformative technologies, like AI today, can completely reshape industries.

Founding Ukibi, the equivalent of LinkedIn five years before LinkedIn, taught me two crucial lessons: timing is everything, and innovation isn't just about creativity, but follows a playbook. Both of these insights are equally true in today's AI-driven world.

While the importance of timing could fill volumes, here I'll focus on the second point.

90

If you're wondering why I've chosen to apply innovation models to explore AI's impact on jobs, let me to take you through the reasoning behind this approach.

Using models to help us think in a structured way

For over a decade, I worked in banking, where one key lesson became clear: we can predict the future. Not always, not with a high degree of precision of course. But with the right model, and by understanding the underlying dynamics of the system, we can identify what's important to be sufficiently prepared.

Financial modelling may sound abstract, but think of it like the storylines in films such as Too Big to Fail or Margin Call — where some players foresaw the subprime crisis. My team and I applied similar models to anticipate the global financial crisis.

While you can't always predict the future with certainty, **building a model helps you focus on what's truly important**, giving you a structured way of thinking and breaking down a complex problem.

This brings us to AI and its impact on jobs. As I began studying AI's role in employment, I came across countless studies predicting large-scale transformations — estimates of how many jobs will be impacted, or the percentage of tasks AI will automate. But these forecasts, while helpful, felt incomplete. They're like predicting that the Earth will warm by 1.5 degrees: useful, yes, but without understanding how the warming will occur, we lack the tools to intervene and influence outcomes.

Rather than just looking at the numbers, I wanted to dive deeper into how this shift would happen. How will AI transform jobs? What is the mechanism that explains the impact of AI on a specific job? What will be the positive or negative effects? And through this process, I realised that the patterns of change closely mirrored an innovation model I've used for years — the **CDE Innovation Prism**.

Understanding technology's impact from the disruptor lens

The CDE Innovation Prism categorises innovations into three types: **Cheaper/Better/Faster (C)**, **Different (D)**, and **Enhancing (E)**. These categories capture the strategies that disruptors use to reshape industries. They also reflect the way that new entrants – the disruptors – think, how they approach a new market, and the likely outcomes.

Why is this perspective of the disruptor important? Consider the following example: when examining the impact of the Internet on traditional media, we could start by looking at it from the newspapers' standpoint. This is useful, but to truly understand the change, we need to focus on the **dynamics created by the Internet itself**, including all the new entrants, and the strategies they followed.

In this chapter, I'll walk you through the **CDE Prism** and show how it helps predict the impacts of technological innovation. To bring the model to life, we'll look at three companies — Amazon, Facebook, and Salesforce — each representing a different type of innovation. By exploring their journeys, we'll identify recurring patterns and use these insights to understand what AI might do to the future of work.

This chapter explores the patterns of technological transformation. If you're keen to dive deeper, I recommend spending time on the case studies at the end, as they provide interesting insights into how to use the CDE Prism. However, if you prefer to get straight to understanding AI's impact on jobs, feel free to skip this part and jump to the next chapter, where we'll apply the **CDE Prism** directly to the **AI-fication of jobs**.

But first, let's explore how innovation itself works through the examples of Amazon, Facebook and Salesforce.

Cheaper, Better, Faster: The Amazon Playbook

In 1994, Jeff Bezos was a senior vice president at D.E. Shaw, a Wall Street hedge fund, with a promising career. But then he came across a statistic that changed his life: Internet usage was growing by 2,300% annually. Recognising the transformative potential, Bezos saw an opportunity to create an online retail business that could scale globally.

This wasn't a decision he took lightly. To decide, Bezos used his "Regret Minimisation Framework." He imagined himself at 80, looking back on his life, and asked if he would regret not acting on the opportunity. The answer was clear — he would regret missing the Internet revolution. With this mindset, he left his secure job and moved to Seattle to build Amazon.

Seattle was a strategic choice, being close to major book distributors like Ingram, which simplified logistics. After analysing 20 different product categories like CDs and electronics, Bezos settled on books, a product with wide appeal and millions of titles. In July 1995, Amazon.com launched from Bezos's garage. At first, it was an online bookshop, offering a massive selection that traditional stores couldn't match. Amazon's key advantage was the ability to offer nearly unlimited shelf space compared to the 100,000 titles typical bookstores could stock.

To compete, Bezos' strategy was to **compete** with established retailers like Barnes and Noble by making Amazon's product offering **cheaper**, **better**, and **faster**. One way Amazon kept prices low was by eliminating the costs associated with physical storefronts.

From the start, Amazon offered significant discounts, selling books up to 40% below retail. As the company grew, it gained leverage with suppliers, securing better deals and further reducing prices.

But low prices weren't enough. Amazon also provided a better shopping experience, allowing customers to find and buy books more easily. Its vast selection, coupled with features like customer reviews and personalised recommendations, offered a customised shopping experience unmatched by physical stores.

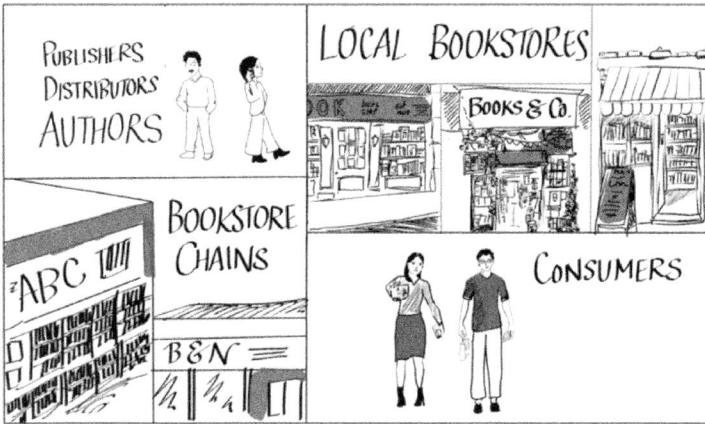

PRE - AMAZONIFICATION

Speed was also crucial. Bezos invested heavily in logistics to allow for faster shipping, and in 2005, the introduction of Amazon Prime, a subscription service offering free two-day delivery, revolutionised the company's ability to deliver quickly.

Bezos always envisioned Amazon expanding beyond books. By the late 1990s, the company added products like CDs, DVDs, and electronics, and in 2000, Amazon Marketplace launched, allowing third-party sellers to list their products. This was a turning point, transforming Amazon into a comprehensive e-commerce platform.

The story of Amazon is a textbook example of how technological innovation — here, the Internet — led to cheaper, better, and faster products. This model of constant improvement is one many companies emulate today. This is also a model that AI is set to follow, offering cheaper, better, and faster products and services.

Cheaper, better, faster than what? Than the incumbents, i.e. humans.

We will explore how AI leverages this Cheaper/Better/Faster framework in the next chapter. But first, let's continue our journey, and look at Facebook which took a radically different approach from Amazon.

Creating a Different World: Facebook

A decade after Bezos left D.E. Shaw, Mark Zuckerberg was a second-year student at Harvard University. A natural programmer from a young age, Zuckerberg launched his first messaging system, ZuckNet, at just 12 years old. In October

2003, he created Facemash, a site that allowed users to vote on the attractiveness of Harvard female students. Controversial and based on unauthorised photos, Facemash was quickly shut down, and Zuckerberg faced disciplinary action.

Months later, in February 2004, Zuckerberg launched The Facebook, a social networking site exclusive to Harvard students. It allowed users to create profiles, upload photos, and connect with classmates. What started as a simple social platform for students became, within a month, an integral part of Harvard's social fabric, with over half the student body signing up. By 2006, Facebook had opened to the general public, and by 2007, it had grown to 60 million users globally.

Facebook's growth was fuelled by network effects — the more people who joined, the more valuable the platform became. The introduction of the News Feed in 2006 turned Facebook into a real-time stream of updates, enhancing engagement. Over time, Facebook expanded beyond social networking, acquiring Instagram and WhatsApp while introducing tools like Messenger.

Facebook didn't just digitise existing social connections — it created a **completely new** digital space for people to build permanent identities and maintain networks across geographical boundaries. Its innovative use of data, particularly through personalised recommendations, transformed how users interacted with each other and the platform. Although initially focused on growth rather than monetisation, Facebook later introduced data-driven advertising, leveraging vast user data to provide targeted ads.

While Cheaper/Better/Faster innovation focuses on refining existing products, "Different" innovation such as Facebook is about creating entirely new spaces and ecosystems. Facebook didn't compete with traditional communication platforms — it built a new digital world that didn't exist before.

Facebook's transformation of social interaction didn't come without controversy. Its reach raised complex ethical questions — about privacy, misinformation, and the impact of social media on mental health — issues that didn't exist in traditional communication methods. This highlights one of the challenges of 'Different' innovation: it introduces new opportunities, but also unprecedented risks.

This type of Different innovation offers a glimpse of how AI could create entirely new industries or ecosystems. Just as Facebook built a new form of global communication, AI could drive the creation of industries that we haven't yet imagined — enabling us to think beyond the existing frameworks of products or services.

Facebook illustrates a type of "Different" innovation, we'll now explore another type of innovation – Enhancing – through the example of Salesforce. Rather than creating something totally different, Salesforce supported others by making them more efficient and effective.

Enhancing Other Businesses: Salesforce

In the late 1990s, Marc Benioff saw how traditional Customer Relationship Management (CRM) systems were expensive, complex, and typically accessible only to large enterprises. He envisioned a cloud-based CRM that would be available to companies of all sizes. In 1999, he founded **Salesforce**, offering CRM accessible to small and medium-sized businesses through the cloud.

Unlike Facebook's creation of a new digital ecosystem, Salesforce's innovation focused on **enhancing** existing business processes. It didn't reinvent customer relationship management but transformed how businesses operated by making CRM tools more accessible, flexible, and scalable.

Salesforce's marketing approach emphasised how the platform empowered clients to build stronger customer relationships, improve productivity, and drive growth.

Salesforce presented itself as a tool that would help businesses work smarter by automating mundane tasks, enabling teams to focus on customer interactions, and providing a unified view of customer data to make better-informed decisions. By centralising information and breaking down silos, Salesforce enabled collaboration across departments, all while scaling flexibly to meet each client's evolving needs.

By automating tasks like follow-ups and lead management, Salesforce freed up sales teams to focus on building relationships rather than handling administrative work. As the platform grew, Salesforce introduced products like Sales Cloud, Service Cloud, and AppExchange, a marketplace for third-party apps, allowing clients to tailor the platform to their unique needs and ultimately become more efficient and productive.

By making CRM systems not only more accessible but also easier to implement and scale, Salesforce allowed smaller businesses to compete on par with larger enterprises, levelling the playing field. This type of **Enhancing innovation** reduced barriers to entry and gave businesses of all sizes the tools they needed to stay competitive.

This type of Enhancing innovation offers a glimpse into how AI could enhance both businesses and individuals. Just as Salesforce empowered businesses by streamlining operations and unlocking new efficiencies, AI has the potential to be a tool that extends human capabilities. Beyond automating repetitive tasks, AI can facilitate complex decision-making, personalise customer experiences, or enable organisations to respond faster to changing market demands. In this way, AI can empower people to focus on higher-value activities, fostering creativity, strategic thinking, and innovation.

Introducing the CDE Innovation Prism

Amazon grew by competing with bookshops, leveraging the Internet to offer a **cheaper, better, and faster** way to buy books.

Facebook built a new and **different** type of product that didn't exist before, completely transforming the way we communicate and behave online.

Salesforce developed a product that **enhanced** its customers' productivity and helped businesses grow by optimising their employees' work.

These three companies represent the different facets of the **CDE Innovation Prism**, which stands for **Cheaper/Better/Faster**, **Different**, and **Enhancing**.

I first developed this framework 10 years ago when trying to explain Fintech's potential to my colleagues in banking, many of whom had little background in technology or innovation. At the time, hundreds of Fintech startups were leveraging technology to disrupt financial services — whether neobanks, peer-to-peer lending, Bitcoin, or robo-advisory services. While these innovations seemed similar, they had fundamentally different characteristics in how they disrupted existing players and altered the dynamics within the industry.

My initial framework categorised innovations into two categories: Cheaper/Better/Faster and Different. This helped tens of thousands of professionals to understand how innovative companies were following a pattern of *Amazonification* or *Facebookisation.*

Recently, I added **Enhancing** to capture innovations that improve existing processes without fully reinventing them (what I call *Salesforcisation,* though I admit it doesn't sound as catchy!). The framework continues to evolve, just as the nature of innovation does.

99

The CDE Innovation Prism focuses on the **dynamics** between **disruptors (new entrants)**, **incumbents (existing suppliers)**, and **customers**. By examining how these three groups interact within the innovation ecosystem, the model provides a way to understand how new technologies reshape industries and force competitors to adapt or fall behind.

The Prism is particularly effective at simplifying complex technological shifts, making it easier to identify trends and anticipate the impact of innovation. Its strength lies in its ability to categorise different innovations based on how they impact the market, helping us see which innovations will improve existing systems and which will create entirely new ones.

Different Types of Innovation Frameworks

There are many other ways to think about innovation, and different frameworks approach this topic from various perspectives. Some focus on the types of innovation, others on how innovation happens, why organisations innovate, the dynamics of how innovations unfold, and the impact on industries and society.

Categorising innovation

Some frameworks classify innovations based on their nature. For example, the **Henderson-Clark Innovation Model** distinguishes between incremental changes and those that fundamentally alter the structure of a product. Similarly, **Blue Ocean Strategy** encourages businesses to innovate by finding new, uncontested markets (blue oceans) instead of competing in crowded, competitive spaces (red oceans).

Helping to innovate

Other frameworks focus on the process of bringing innovations to life. The **Business Model Canvas**, for instance, helps innovators map out their entire business idea in a simple, visual format — covering customer segments, revenue streams, and resources. **Lean Canvas** and **Design Thinking** offer additional structures to turn ideas into reality by testing them, gathering feedback, and making quick adjustments.

Understanding why

Understanding why we innovate is as important as knowing how. The **Jobs-to-be-Done** theory shifts the focus from the product to the customer's needs, asking, "What job is this product helping the customer accomplish?" This approach uncovers the deeper motivations behind customer choices. Simon Sinek's **Golden Circle** similarly encourages innovators to start with their purpose — focusing on the core mission behind creating new products or services.

Understanding how innovation progresses

Frameworks like **Everett Rogers' Diffusion of Innovations** explain how innovations spread from early adopters to the mainstream, while the Gartner Hype Cycle shows how new technologies often pass through phases of initial excitement, disappointment, and eventual widespread adoption. These models help us understand how innovations gain momentum and reach the broader market.

Identifying the impact of innovation

Some frameworks focus on the impact of innovation on industries and society. **Clayton Christensen's Disruptive Innovation** framework shows how innovations can upend entire industries by displacing established players, while **Scenario Planning**, developed by Peter Schwartz, explores multiple future outcomes, helping organisations anticipate the long-term effects of innovation.

All the approaches mentioned above are very useful for understanding different aspects of innovation. With my background in business and entrepreneurship, my main interest has always been to "predict the future" — in other words, to forecast trends and assign probabilities to likely scenarios. This is why I created the **CDE Innovation Prism**, with a focus on the dynamics between disruptors, incumbents, and customers. By examining these relationships, the model shows how **new entrants challenge existing players, how incumbents respond, and how customer preferences evolve in the process.**

This makes the **CDE Prism** particularly effective for understanding how innovations — such as AI — will reshape industries. Let's dive deeper into what it is, and how to apply it.

Defining the CDE Innovation Prism

THE CDE MODEL

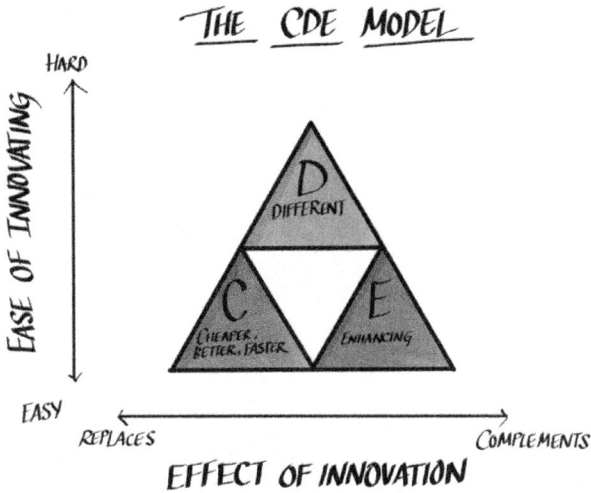

The **CDE Innovation Prism** is a framework designed to categorise and understand different types of innovations based on their core characteristics and their impact on various stakeholders, including disruptors, incumbents, and customers. It breaks innovations into three key types:

- **Cheaper/Better/Faster (C)**,
- **Different (D)**,
- and **Enhancing (E)**.

Each type represents a distinct way innovations influence and transform products, services, and ecosystems.

Cheaper/Better/Faster (C) Innovations:

These innovations focus on making existing products or services more affordable, efficient, or accessible. They typically involve incremental improvements that reduce costs or improve performance, enabling companies to compete on price and efficiency in established markets.

Examples:

- **Amazon**: Amazon made online retail cheaper and more efficient by reducing the need for physical storefronts and using vast logistics networks to cut shipping costs and improve delivery times. This focus on cost-cutting and operational efficiency revolutionised the retail industry.
- **Low-Cost Airlines:** Carriers like **Ryanair** and **AirAsia** reshaped air travel by eliminating unnecessary amenities and optimising operations to offer significantly lower fares, making air travel more accessible to the broader public.
- **Chinese Smartphone Manufacturers** (e.g., **Xiaomi**): Xiaomi disrupted the smartphone industry by offering high-quality devices with advanced features at much lower prices than competitors like Apple or Samsung. By cutting production costs and selling directly online, they made smartphones more affordable for emerging markets.

Different (D) Innovations

Different innovations create entirely new markets or categories. These innovations don't compete directly with existing solutions but instead bring something fundamentally new, reshaping consumer behaviour and opening up fresh market spaces.

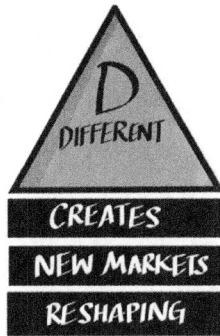

Examples:

- **Facebook**: Facebook created a new way for people to connect and communicate online, establishing a completely different kind of social network. It transformed how people interact globally, creating the social media industry.
- **iPhone**: Apple's iPhone wasn't just an improvement on existing phones — it redefined what a phone could be by integrating a touchscreen and an app ecosystem, creating the smartphone category.
- **Netflix**: Netflix didn't just improve the DVD rental model — it changed how people consumed media by launching an on-demand streaming platform, disrupting traditional television and film industries.

Enhancing (E) Innovations

Enhancing innovations improve the performance of existing products, services, or employees. These innovations provide tools or enhancements that allow users to work more effectively, expanding the value of existing offerings.

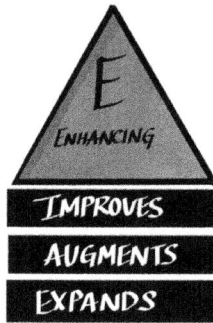

Examples:

- **Salesforce**: Salesforce enhances how businesses manage customer relationships by automating workflows and providing data-driven insights, helping businesses be more effective without replacing existing operations.
- **Zoom**: Zoom enhanced communication by offering a cloud-based video conferencing platform that improved the way people conduct meetings without replacing existing tools.
- **Shopify**: Shopify empowers businesses of all sizes to easily set up and run online stores. It enhances traditional commerce by offering integrated tools for managing e-commerce, payments, and logistics.

Purpose of the CDE Innovation Prism

The CDE Innovation Prism helps to categorise innovation, but also to predict how markets will evolve by identifying the dynamics between disruptors, incumbents, and customers. By understanding these interactions, we can better anticipate how innovations will unfold and reshape industries.

The CDE Prism allows us to analyse three key aspects:

- **The Type of Innovation**: Does the innovation improve existing products, create something new, or enhance current capabilities?
- **The Dynamics of Innovation**: How do disruptors challenge incumbents, how do incumbents respond, and how do customers adapt?
- **The Impact on the Market**: How do clients, employees, industries, and markets experience and respond to these innovations?

By categorising innovations this way, the **CDE Innovation Prism** offers a comprehensive perspective on how innovations unfold, helping policymakers, industry leaders, and individuals better understand and anticipate the effects of innovation on their sectors.

Structure of the CDE Innovation Prism

To analyse how companies evolve through the lens of the CDE Innovation Prism, we use the **EDGE canvas**, which focuses on four key aspects: **Existing Ecosystem**, **Disruptor**, **Game Plan**, and **End Result**. This structure helps us assess not just the innovation itself but also its effect on industries, competitors, and broader market dynamics.

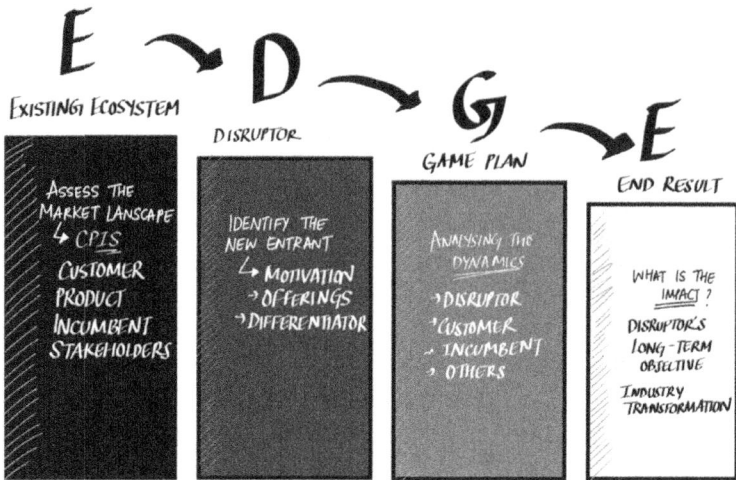

The **EDGE canvas** helps us analyse the journey of disruption within the context of the **CDE Innovation Prism**. By examining each phase — **Existing Ecosystem**, **Disruptor**, **Game Plan**, and **End Result** — we can understand how innovations categorised as Cheaper/Better/Faster, Different, or Enhancing unfold and impact industries. Each part of the EDGE canvas represents a phase in the innovation journey, starting with current market conditions, then showing how a disruptor enters, and finally, how that disruptor's innovation transforms the market and impacts various stakeholders.

1. Existing Ecosystem

The **Existing Ecosystem** is the foundation of any industry before the innovation occurs. It includes the established products, services, incumbents, and customers who maintain the current industry structure.

Understanding the existing ecosystem is essential because it highlights inefficiencies and unmet customer needs that disruptors can capitalise on. This foundation allows us to see where opportunities for innovation lie and helps predict how a disruptor might impact the current players and practices.

Take **Netflix** as an example. Before Netflix revolutionised media consumption with its streaming platform, the existing ecosystem for entertainment consisted of traditional television networks and DVD rentals, dominated by companies like **Blockbuster**. Customers had to rent physical DVDs or watch TV according to fixed schedules. This system was slow, limited in choice, and heavily reliant on physical locations or broadcast schedules.

Similarly, **low-cost airlines** like **Ryanair** and **AirAsia** entered a market where traditional airlines ruled, offering full-service flights at high prices. The ecosystem prioritised comfort and amenities over affordability, leaving a gap for cost-conscious flyers.

Key elements of the existing ecosystem include:

- **Customers**: Who are the current clients, and how are their needs being met? For Netflix, customers were renting DVDs or watching TV according to schedules. For low-cost airlines, most customers were either paying for expensive full-service flights or not flying at all due to high prices.
- **Products/Services**: What offerings dominate the market? For airlines, full-service flights dominated. For Netflix, it was physical media rentals and cable television.

- **Incumbents**: The major players, like Blockbuster for video rentals or legacy airlines for air travel, who dominated before disruption.

THE INCUMBENT IN THE EXISTING ECOSYSTEM

- **Other Stakeholders**: There can be many different other stakeholders, such as distributors, regulators, and partners who are important for the market to function.

2. Disruptor

The **Disruptor** introduces a new element into the existing ecosystem. It's a company that brings an innovative product, service, or business model that challenges or changes the established dynamics. The disruptor often identifies inefficiencies, unmet needs, or opportunities the current ecosystem isn't addressing.

Take **Apple's iPhone** as an example. Before the iPhone, the mobile phone market was dominated by phones with limited functionality or professional devices like BlackBerry. Apple identified an opportunity to create a device that combined communication, entertainment, and Internet browsing into one sleek product. The iPhone redefined what a phone could do and reshaped customer expectations, launching an entire ecosystem of apps.

110

Amazon similarly disrupted retail by transitioning book buying to an online platform. Brick-and-mortar bookstores like **Barnes & Noble** struggled with inventory and physical limitations. Amazon used the Internet to offer virtually unlimited selection, transforming how people shop not only for books but eventually for nearly everything.

Disruptors often:

- **Identify inefficiencies or unmet needs**: Apple saw the limitations of mobile devices, and Amazon identified constraints in physical bookshops.
- **Introduce innovations that challenge current norms**: Apple introduced a touchscreen smartphone with apps, and Amazon offered a limitless e-commerce platform.
- **Shift customer behaviour**: Both Apple and Amazon changed how consumers interacted with their products, whether through smartphones or online shopping.

3. Game Plan (Dynamics)

The **Game Plan** refers to how the disruptor executes its strategy after entering the market. It includes how they position their product, attract customers, navigate competition, and how incumbents and the market react to the disruption.

For example:

- **Apple** positioned the **iPhone** as a premium product and created an ecosystem of apps to lock in customer loyalty. Incumbents like BlackBerry initially downplayed the iPhone, focusing on physical keyboards. Their delayed reaction led to their rapid decline.
- **Amazon** disrupted retail with aggressive pricing and logistical efficiency. Incumbents like Borders and Barnes & Noble reacted in different ways, some built their own online platforms, some partnered, others changed their market strategy.

Key aspects of a game plan include:

- **Positioning**: How the disruptor positions its product against existing market offerings, emphasising convenience or superior functionality.
- **Customer Acquisition:** The strategy a disruptor uses to gain new clients, recognising that customers — whether individuals or businesses — are often resistant to changing their habits and adopting new products.
- **Incumbent Response**: Incumbents are likely to react to a disruptor's actions, either by downplaying the disruptor, replicating its innovations, or developing new competitive strategies.
- **Market Reactions:** The broader market may adopt new norms introduced by the disruptor, as seen with smartphones and e-commerce.

4. End Result (Impact)

The **End Result** is the lasting impact of the disruptor's innovation. This reflects how the market evolves, customer preferences shift, and industry norms change due to the disruption.

For example:

- **Apple's iPhone** not only dominated the smartphone market but fundamentally changed how we interact with technology. It gave rise to the app economy and reshaped industries like gaming and social media.
- **Amazon** transformed retail and logistics, influencing adjacent industries and creating new expectations around convenience and pricing.

In this phase, we observe:

- **Shifts in the market** and market shares as disruptors reshape the ecosystem.

112

- **Changes in customer preferences** as they adapt to new offerings.
- **Creation of new ecosystems**, such as the app economy (Apple) or the e-commerce supply chain (Amazon).

Applying the EDGE Canvas Across Different Types of Disruption

The EDGE Canvas applies equally well to different types of innovations — whether Amazon's **Cheaper/Better/Faster** approach, Apple's iPhone as a **Different** innovation, or Shopify's **Enhancing** proposition for e-commerce. This flexibility makes it a useful tool for understanding how each innovation type impacts the market and reshapes industries.

Predicting the Future with the CDE Innovation Prism

Based on my experience with innovation models, I've noticed that **Cheaper/Better/Faster (C)**, **Different (D)**, and **Enhancing (E)** innovations each follow unique patterns and have distinct impacts on their industries.

To make this more concrete, let's walk through each type of innovation. If this feels abstract, try this mental exercise: think of a company that fits each category. As we go along, check whether they align with the patterns I'm about to describe — you'll likely see that many innovations follow these paths.

Cheaper, Better, Faster (C) Innovations

The disruptors unbundle, grow, and rebundle — if they make it

In the CDE Prism, **Cheaper/Better/Faster (C)** innovations focus on **competing with incumbents by offering more efficient or affordable alternatives**. Disruptors typically begin by identifying inefficiencies or gaps in the market where existing players fall short. They capitalise on these weaknesses by offering a Cheaper, Better, Faster solution, often by focusing on a single vertical — a strategy known as **unbundling**. This allows them to zero in on one area where they can outperform incumbents, such as Amazon initially focusing solely on books.

CHEAPER, BETTER & FASTER

For example, in financial services, Fintech startups often target specific functions like payments, currency transfers, or investing. This focused approach enables them to deliver streamlined, superior experiences. However, this narrow focus

114

makes it a highly competitive space, with many startups vying for the same niche. While disruptors can grow quickly by solving these specific inefficiencies, they must compete both with incumbents and other disruptors, making survival in the early stages a challenge.

During the unbundling phase, disruptors typically follow straightforward business models. They compete directly with incumbents by offering better pricing or more efficient services, using clear-cut, scalable revenue streams. This simplicity is an advantage early on, allowing them to quickly deliver value within an established structure.

However, as disruptors grow, they face a new challenge: limited profitability due to their narrow product focus. To sustain growth, they often begin **rebundling** — expanding their offerings to include more products or services. This expansion is critical for achieving economies of scale and unlocking cross-selling opportunities. For instance, Amazon started with books but eventually expanded into a full e-commerce platform, dominating various categories.

While many disruptors start with similar ambitions, only a few manage to scale successfully. Predicting which companies will follow in Amazon's footsteps is tricky   many will fail. But those that do succeed often achieve a winner-takes-all position, making it nearly impossible for competitors to challenge them.

Incumbents

Initially, incumbents are often slow to react, especially when disruptors offer simpler, more limited products. Established companies rely on their brand strength and broader product suites, which many customers prefer for convenience. However, as disruptors gain momentum and attract early adopters, incumbents start to feel the pressure.

Disruptors force incumbents to compete on price, quality, or speed, as customers now have more options. This can push incumbents to innovate — lowering prices, enhancing service quality, or speeding up delivery. Those who adapt quickly often thrive, using the competition to refine their offerings.

But incumbents that fail to respond risk irrelevance. They face a crucial decision: innovate to match the disruptor's improvements or lose market share. Incumbents who resist change often decline as customers migrate to more innovative solutions.

Customers

Not all customers immediately embrace new entrants. Many remain loyal to incumbents, especially if the incumbent offers a broad range of services or has built up trust over time. However, early adopters — tech-savvy, adventurous, or price-conscious — are the first to try new products that promise better pricing, speed, or functionality.

As disruptors improve their offerings, more customers take notice. When the new products prove reliable and offer clear benefits, the wider market starts to adopt them, increasing the disruptor's market share. Over time, customers benefit from increased competition, enjoying lower prices, improved quality, and faster service.

Even those who stay with incumbents experience the ripple effect, as incumbents are forced to raise their standards, resulting in a more dynamic marketplace with enhanced choices and products.

Summary of Cheaper/Better/Faster Dynamics

Cheaper, Better, Faster (C) innovations follow a predictable pattern:

1. **Disruptors unbundle** by focusing on a niche, and as they grow, they **rebundle** to expand their offerings and drive profitability.

116

2. **Incumbents** often underestimate the threat but are forced to innovate as competition intensifies. Those who adapt grow stronger, while others become obsolete.
3. **Customers** benefit from increased competition, enjoying lower prices, better quality, and faster service.

In conclusion, **Cheaper, Better, Faster** innovations drive competition by challenging incumbents on price, efficiency, and speed. Key concepts here are *incremental improvement, competitiveness,* and *performance.* Innovations in this category aim to outpace established players, often by leveraging superior digital capabilities and streamlined experiences. As disruptors grow and become incumbents themselves, the cycle repeats with new challengers entering the market to push innovation further.

1. UNBUNDLING

2. COMPETITION 2

3. WINNER-TAKES-ALL

4. REBUNDLING

Different (D) Innovations

Disruptors in the **Different** category don't aim to compete with incumbents, but they often have a **vision of a completely new world,** driven by the potential to change behaviours, experiences, or entire industries. These are the entrepreneurs who see what doesn't yet exist and create something fundamentally novel. Because they operate outside familiar frameworks, they often lack clear business models initially. Their innovations don't fit neatly into established categories, making it difficult to predict how they'll generate revenue or evolve.

Different innovations are much less common than **Cheaper/Better/Faster** ones. Most people think in terms of incremental improvements, but this approach requires a willingness to explore uncharted territory and envision possibilities others may not yet see. These innovations come with a high degree of uncertainty, making them riskier investments. Achieving **product-market fit** and creating a sustainable **business model** is particularly challenging, as there are no direct comparables or existing revenue streams to build on.

Product innovation is central to **Different** disruptors. These innovations push boundaries, introducing entirely new products or services that transform how we interact with technology or each other. However, this uniqueness can also be a double-edged sword. Some disruptors fail due to lack of demand or the inability to monetise their innovations.

Yet, for those disruptors that succeed, the rewards are transformative: they can redefine industries or create new ones. Take **Facebook** and **Google** as examples. Both started as niche platforms with unique functionalities but eventually reshaped global industries. **Facebook** built the ecosystem of social media, while **Google's** search engine became the backbone of digital marketing — a multi-billion-dollar industry. In both cases, these disruptors fundamentally changed how people connect, search, and interact with information, with an impact on billions of people.

Customers

For **Different** innovations, early adoption is driven by **innovators and pioneers** — customers who are eager to try new things and drawn to the product's novelty. These early adopters don't just use the product — they often become deeply invested, helping to shape its growth and creating communities around it. Early users of **Facebook** and **Google** provided valuable feedback that contributed to the platforms' evolution, and their enthusiasm helped drive broader adoption.

As the product develops, the next phase depends on whether it resonates with a wider audience. In some cases, **Different** innovations gain mainstream adoption, becoming part of everyday life for millions. In other cases, they remain niche, appealing to a smaller group of dedicated enthusiasts. Regardless, these innovations foster strong community dynamics, with early adopters acting as **evangelists** who bring others on board.

Whether they go mainstream or remain niche, **Different** innovations offer customers entirely new experiences and choices, introducing novel ways of engaging with the world that didn't previously exist.

Incumbents

At first, incumbents may not see **Different** innovations as a direct threat, as these new products often target markets or customers that incumbents haven't considered. However, as **Different** innovations gain traction and create new ecosystems, incumbents start to feel competitive pressure.

For example, the rise **of social media led** to the growth of complementary services like digital advertising and influencer marketing. The iPhone didn't just disrupt mobile phones — it transformed industries from software development to digital content delivery, leading to the rise of the App Store ecosystem.

Once the ecosystem takes hold, incumbents must adapt or risk irrelevance. Traditional phone makers like Nokia and BlackBerry initially dismissed the iPhone, but soon found themselves outcompeted. Similarly, Facebook and Twitter disrupted traditional media companies, capturing user attention for news and information. Incumbents that pivot and participate in these ecosystems can grow, but those unable to adapt face significant risks as **Different** innovations can render traditional business models obsolete.

Summary of Different Dynamics

Different (D) innovations follow a unique and **unpredictable** path:

1. **Disruptors** start with a vision, launching a product without a proven business model. They aim for transformation, not incremental improvement, and face high uncertainty and significant risk. If successful, they create or redefine entire industries.
2. **Customers** are initially **innovators** and **early adopters**, attracted by the novelty. These pioneers help build communities and fuel growth. The innovation may go mainstream or remain niche, but either way, it offers entirely new choices for customers.
3. **Incumbents** may not see the disruptor as a competitor at first, but as the new ecosystem grows, incumbents face competitive pressure. Some incumbents thrive by adapting, while others risk irrelevance as the **Different** innovation reshapes markets.

In conclusion, **Different** innovations can redefine – or create – products or event industries and markets. Key terms to consider here are *disruption, transformation,* and *revolution*. Innovations that embody these elements break with traditional models, establishing fresh landscapes and fundamentally reshaping industries.

I. VISION

II. PRODUCT INNOVATION

III. FIND BUSINESS MODEL

IV. UNPREDICTIBLE OUTCOME

Enhancing (E) Innovations

Disruptors

Disruptors in the **Enhancing** category don't aim to replace existing products or create something entirely new. Instead, they focus on **improving** how businesses or individuals perform tasks, whether by boosting productivity, increasing efficiency, or enhancing accessibility. These disruptors provide tools that help customers operate more effectively, making previously inaccessible capabilities available to a broader audience.

For example, Microsoft Office has continuously enhanced workplace productivity by providing tools like Word, Excel, and PowerPoint, which allow individuals and businesses to perform essential tasks with greater speed and precision. Over time, these tools evolved into cloud-based solutions like Microsoft 365, enabling real-time collaboration, task automation, and remote access. These enhancements help users to do their jobs more efficiently without fundamentally changing the nature of the work itself.

ENHANCING

Enhancing disruptors often begin by **unbundling**, offering focused solutions that address a specific need. As they grow, they **rebundle** by adding complementary features or products, expanding into a comprehensive suite. Microsoft Office, for instance, expanded from basic word processing and spreadsheets to advanced tools for collaboration, data analysis, and cloud storage. This rebundling generates new revenue streams and builds customer loyalty, much like Cheaper, Better, Faster disruptors. Unbundling and Rebundling is similar in both Cheaper/Better/Faster and Enhancing, because it's much easier for new entrants to start on a niche.

The ultimate goal of **Enhancing** disruptors is to become indispensable partners for their customers. By continuously improving the tools they offer, they create deep integration with their clients, helping them achieve better results and stay competitive in their industries.

Incumbents

For incumbents, the arrival of **Enhancing** disruptors is often a positive development. Instead of replacing incumbents, these new entrants provide tools that improve existing operations, making incumbents more competitive. By adopting these innovations, incumbents can increase productivity, boost efficiency, and, in some cases, better compete with Cheaper, Better, Faster disruptors.

For instance, an established bank might adopt a Fintech platform that automates compliance tasks, reducing overhead and increasing operational efficiency. Similarly, traditional retailers could use data analytics tools to optimise their supply chains or personalise customer interactions. In these cases, **Enhancing** innovations reinforce incumbents' positions, helping them adapt to changing conditions while remaining competitive.

For incumbents that successfully integrate these tools, **Enhancing** innovations can drive internal transformation, helping them adopt more agile business practices. However, incumbents that fail to embrace these technologies may fall behind, as competitors who adopt them become more agile and responsive to market demands.

Customers

Customers of incumbents may not immediately notice the impact of **Enhancing** innovations, as these improvements often operate behind the scenes. However, they still benefit indirectly, as incumbents use these tools to improve their services. For example, a bank that adopts a more efficient loan processing system can offer faster approvals, while a retailer using inventory management software can ensure products are consistently in stock.

Ultimately, **Enhancing** innovations allow incumbents to deliver **Cheaper, Better, Faster** services to their customers. While the tools themselves may be invisible to the end user, customers experience the benefits through improved service quality, quicker turnaround times, and sometimes lower costs. Over time, these enhancements become part of customers' expectations, pushing incumbents to continue adopting new tools to stay competitive and meet rising demands.

Summary of Enhancing Dynamics

Enhancing (E) innovations follow a distinct development path:

1. **Disruptors** begin by targeting specific customers — often enterprises — and create tools that enhance **productivity**, **efficiency**, and **accessibility**. They typically start with a **focused offering** (unbundling) and expand over time into a comprehensive suite (rebundling), aiming to become an integral part of their customers' operations.
2. **Incumbents** benefit from adopting **Enhancing** innovations, as these tools improve their competitiveness, enabling them to better respond to market challenges. By incorporating these innovations, incumbents are empowered to compete more effectively with **Cheaper, Better, Faster** disruptors.
3. **Customers** of incumbents may not directly interact with these tools but experience the benefits indirectly. As

incumbents adopt **Enhancing** innovations, they deliver **improved services**, offering faster, more efficient, and often more affordable solutions that meet evolving customer expectations.

In conclusion, **Enhancing** innovations strengthen the broader ecosystem by supporting established players to improve performance and adapt to evolving demands. Think of keywords like *productivity, augmentation, optimisation or improvement.* Innovations that fall within these categories would typically follow the **Enhancing** playbook.

I. UNBUNDLING

II. ENTERPRISE SALES

III. LONG SALES CYCLE

IV. REBUNDLING

Conclusion: the CDE Prism is a powerful and simple model to understand innovation dynamics

In this chapter, we explored the CDE Innovation Prism, a structured framework designed to categorise and understand how different types of innovations emerge and reshape industries. By examining **Cheaper/Better/Faster (C), Different (D), and Enhancing (E)** innovations, we can better predict how AI will impact industries, jobs, and society at large.

Each type of innovation follows distinct patterns:

- **Cheaper/Better/Faster (C)** innovations, like **Amazon**, focus on **incremental improvements** that allow companies to outperform incumbents by competing on cost, efficiency, or speed.
- **Different (D)** innovations, such as **Facebook**, create **entirely new markets** or even ecosystems and industries, potentially impacting a very large number of people quickly.
- **Enhancing (E)** innovations, exemplified by tools like **Salesforce**, improve the **performance** of existing systems, helping businesses and individuals to work more effectively.

However, the real power of the CDE Prism lies not just in categorising innovations but in its ability to model the dynamics between disruptors, incumbents, and customers. This allows us to map out trends and predict how markets will evolve in response to innovation.

Identifying Trends with the CDE Prism

By focusing on these **interactions**, the **CDE Prism** helps us to understand key dynamics such as:

129

- **Competition vs. Collaboration**: The framework clearly delineates how **Cheaper/Better/Faster** innovations often push industries towards competition, forcing incumbents to lower costs and improve efficiency. In contrast, **Enhancing** innovations create opportunities for collaboration, as incumbents can adopt new tools to improve their operations and meet evolving customer needs.
- **Incremental vs. Disruptive Thinking**: The CDE Prism also highlights how innovation is typically driven by incremental improvements in established industries (Cheaper/Better/Faster), which are easier to understand, fund, and implement. In contrast, **Different** innovations are rarer because they require a higher degree of risk-taking and a more visionary approach, often leading to resistance from both investors and consumers.

Common Innovation Patterns

From my experience as a founding partner of **Supercharger**, Asia's largest Fintech accelerator, I've observed that **Cheaper/Better/Faster** strategies are by far the most common among new entrants. Startups often focus on offering more affordable or efficient solutions to existing problems, gaining traction by competing on price or speed. **Enhancing** innovations are also frequently pursued, as they allow businesses to improve productivity without overhauling entire systems.

However, truly disruptive **Different** innovations are **much rarer.** Not only because they require more visionary thinking, but also because they are harder to finance, often lacking a clear business model and needing significant market education to succeed. Different innovations like Facebook or Bitcoin show the immense potential when they do succeed, but the road to success is fraught with uncertainty and higher risk.

How the CDE Prism Helps Us Predict AI's Impact

As we look to the future of work in an AI-driven world, the **CDE Prism** will prove very valuable in anticipating how AI will transform the job market. AI has the potential to operate in each of these categories:

- In a **Cheaper/Better/Faster (C)** model, AI becomes a direct competitor to the Incumbent, in that case the human workforce
- With a **Different (D)** approach, AI could create entirely new sectors or job roles we haven't yet imagined, reshaping industries in ways we cannot fully predict.
- And as an **Enhancing (E)** force, AI will augment human workers, enabling them to achieve more by automating routine tasks and offering smarter decision-making tools.

This framework is particularly useful because it helps us to predict how these transformations will unfold, focusing on the interactions between disruptors, incumbents, and customers. Understanding these dynamics is critical for **policymakers**, **business leaders**, and **individuals** who need to prepare for the future. By mapping out these relationships, the CDE Prism allows us to **anticipate trends** and **mitigate disruptions** while seizing new opportunities.

From predicting to shaping the future

Ultimately, using the CDE Innovation Prism should help us go beyond predicting the future, but it should equip us with the intellectual tools to shape it. By identifying key patterns and understanding the dynamics at play, we can actively influence how AI and other technologies impact society and the workforce.

In the following section, we'll apply the CDE Innovation Prism to Fintech, one of today's most dynamic ecosystems for innovation. Feel free to skip ahead to the impact of AI on jobs, or, if you're interested in innovation, dive in to see how this framework applies to real-world examples such as Revolut, Bitcoin and Stripe.

In the next chapter, we'll analyse the impact of AI on jobs. We've been on quite a journey to get here — thank you, Reader, for your patience, and congratulations on your intellectual persistence!

As we noted early on, understanding AI's effects on jobs from our own perspective is challenging; after all, we're part of the equation as incumbents. Now, with a good framework to predict technological innovation, we're ready to apply these insights to AI and its implications for the workforce.

Case Studies

Applying CDE to Fintech

Fintech has been one of the most vibrant and rapidly evolving sectors, with more than $200 billion invested globally over the last decade. It has transformed how we think about financial services, from banking and payments to lending and insurance. In this section, we will apply the CDE Innovation Prism to three major initiatives in the Fintech space — **Revolut**, **Bitcoin**, and **Stripe** — each representing a different innovation type: **Cheaper/Better/Faster**, **Different**, and **Enhancing**. By examining these companies, we can see how innovation unfolds and reshapes industries using the **EDGE framework,** and how the **CDE prism** predicted some of the trends.

I. Revolut as an example of Cheaper, Better, Faster

You might be one of the 50 million users of Revolut globally. At CFTE, we have used Revolut as an example of Cheaper, Better, Faster since 2017, when they had fewer than 2 million users, because they were a typical example of **Cheaper/Better/Faster**. As an anecdote, CFTE's second office was Revolut's first office at Level39 in London, which provided us with an even closer view of its evolution.

They were founded in London in 2015 with the objective to simplify and reduce the cost of international money transfers. It started as a mobile app offering real-time currency exchange at interbank rates, quickly attracting frequent travellers and users frustrated by the high fees of traditional banks. Following the Cheaper/Better/Faster (C) model of innovation, Revolut positioned itself as a low-cost, high-accessibility alternative to banks and bureaux de change.

Today, Revolut has grown to over **50 million users across almost 50 countries** — and it's a good illustration of the "winner takes all" approach in the Cheaper/Better/Faster model. While other companies, like Brazil's Nubank, have also scaled quickly with similar models, many other Fintechs pursuing cost-focused disruption have struggled to achieve the same traction, underscoring the high-risk, high-reward nature of the approach.

The started with **unbundling** — offering specific services like currency exchange and international payments rather than providing a full-service banking experience. As it grew,

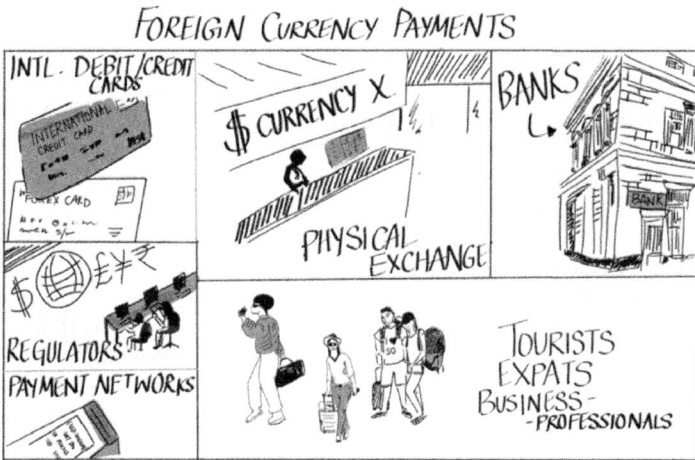

FOREIGN CURRENCY PAYMENTS

Revolut **rebundled** these services, expanding its offerings to include cryptocurrency trading, stock trading, budgeting tools, and even HR services. This transition allowed Revolut to transform into a comprehensive digital financial platform. However, like many disruptors, Revolut has not been without **controversies**; it has faced criticism regarding its corporate culture and questions around profitability, challenges typical of companies prioritising growth over immediate financial returns.

Despite these challenges, the impact on customer expectations and the financial services industry has been significant. By setting new standards for low fees, digital accessibility, and rapid onboarding, neobanks such as Revolut have pushed traditional banks to innovate and elevate their services in response. They have fundamentally reshaped user expectations in financial services, demonstrating the disruptive power of the Cheaper/Better/Faster model in redefining what consumers expect from their financial institutions .

Let's break down Revolut's impact using the EDGE framework.

EDGE Analysis of Revolut

E   D   G   E

1. Existing Ecosystem

E   D   G   E

- **Customers**: Initially, Revolut targeted cost-conscious, tech-savvy individuals who frequently travel or make international payments. These customers were traditionally served by banks that imposed high fees and unfavourable exchange rates on cross-border transactions.

- **Products/Services**: Traditional banks offered foreign exchange and cross-border payment services as part of their larger product suites. However, these services were often expensive, slow, and not tailored to a digital-first experience.

- **Incumbents**: The primary incumbents in this space were large, established banks and bureaux de change. These incumbents typically charged significant fees for currency exchanges and cross-border transactions, relying on legacy infrastructure and physical branches to deliver these services.

- **Other Stakeholders**: The ecosystem included card networks (e.g., Visa, Mastercard), regulatory bodies, and payment processors, all of which played a role in either supporting the growth of Revolut or supervising its activities / granting licenses.

2. Disruptor (New Entrant)

- **Why**: Revolut entered the market to address a specific pain point: the high cost and inefficiency of international payments and currency exchange. Traditional banks offered slow, expensive services that didn't align with the needs of a mobile-first generation looking for cost-effective, instant transactions.

- **What**: Revolut launched with a digital app-based model, offering real-time currency exchange at interbank rates and low-cost international payments. This approach allowed customers to avoid hefty fees while accessing competitive exchange rates and convenient mobile access.

- **How**: By focusing on mobile technology, Revolut provided a seamless, app-based user experience. The company initially focused on unbundling foreign exchange from the broader suite of banking services, allowing it to offer a targeted, more efficient service. Revolut's mobile-first approach also helped it reach customers directly, bypassing the need for physical branches and thus reducing overhead.

3. Game Plan (Dynamics)

- **Disruptor Push**: Revolut's strategy was to scale quickly by acquiring users attracted to its low-cost services. It initially offered competitive exchange rates and free international transactions, which helped build a large user base. Over time, Revolut **rebundled** by adding new features, such as premium accounts, cryptocurrency trading, and budgeting tools, transforming itself into a more comprehensive financial platform.

- **Customer Pull**: Revolut's early adopters were young professionals who travelled frequently, drawn to the low fees for foreign exchange. Revolut quickly embedded viral features — like instant money transfers between users — to encourage customers to share the app with others. This mobile-first, user-centred approach helped Revolut expand in a few years from a niche market to a broader audience.

- **Incumbent Pushback**: Traditional banks felt the competitive pressure as Revolut's user base grew. Many banks responded by lowering fees, investing in digital platforms, and offering more competitive exchange rates. However, their legacy systems often hindered their ability to match Revolut's cost structure and mobile agility.

- **Regulatory and Stakeholder Reactions**: Despite its rapid growth and popularity, Revolut faced regulatory issues, resulting in a 3-year wait for its UK banking licence due to concerns over financial reporting and operational transparency. Credit card networks such as Visa and Mastercard supported Revolut's growth, as its business model benefited their activities.

4. End Result (Impact)

- **Customers**: Customers benefited from more affordable and convenient international payment options, forcing traditional banks to improve their own digital offerings and reduce fees. Revolut and other Fintech startups set a new standard in cost and speed, and in general customer experience for banking.

- **Products**: Revolut started with a focused service, but over time, its product line expanded to include a broad array of financial services, moving from an unbundled to a rebundled offering. This positioned Revolut as a more comprehensive digital financial platform.

- **Incumbents**: Banks that failed to adapt quickly found it challenging to retain customers, especially younger, mobile-first users. Some incumbents responded to the Fintech wave by investing in digital transformations and quickly modernising, while others were constrained by legacy systems.

- **Other Stakeholders**: Card networks and payment processors benefited from Revolut's business model, as it drove transaction volume through their platforms. Regulatory bodies adjusted to new digital banking models, leading to evolving compliance requirements for digital-first financial services.

E	D	G	E
EXISTING ECOSYSTEM	DISRUPTOR	GAME PLAN	END RESULT
CUSTOMER		DISRUPTOR PUSH → SCALE QUICKLY → COMPETITIVE PRICING	🙂 CUSTOMERS → NEW STD. IN COST & SPEED OF INTL. PAYMENTS
COST-CONSCIOUS, TECH-SAVY PEOPLE (TRAVEL OR MAKE INTL PAYMENTS)			
PRODUCT	Revolut	CUSTOMER PULL → AFFORDABILITY → CONVENIENCE → CX & UI ★★★★★	😊 PRODUCT → EXPANDED SUITE → UNBUNDLED → REBUNDLED OFFERING (CRYPTO) ↑↑
FOREIGN EXCHANGE SERVICES	• DIGITAL APP • REAL-TIME EXCHANGE • LOW-COST		
INCUMBENT		INCUMBENT PUSH-BACK → PRICE PRESSURE ↳ LOWERED FEES ↳ DIGITISED → ↓LEGACY SYSTEM	😐 INCUMBENTS → SOME FI's FAILED TO ADOPT QUICKLY → CONSTRAINED BY LEGACY SYSTEMS
LARGE BANKS FINANCIAL INSTITUTIONS			
OTHER STAKEHOLDERS		STAKEHOLDER REACTION → PARTNERSHIPS WITH CARD NETWORKS → COMPLIANCE	🙂 CARD NETWORKS 😐 REGULATORY BODIES
CARD NETWORKS REGULATORY BODIES PAYMENT PROCESSORS			

How Revolut Followed the Cheaper/Better/Faster Pattern

Revolut's business strategy closely aligns with the **Cheaper/Better/Faster** innovation pattern. It entered the financial services market with a focused, unbundled offering — addressing the high costs associated with international payments and currency exchange. By providing real-time foreign exchange at interbank rates and eliminating many of the fees that banks typically charged, Revolut captured a growing base of customers looking for more affordable, transparent solutions.

As Revolut's user base grew, the company moved towards **rebundling**. It added services like budgeting tools, premium accounts, and even cryptocurrency trading,

140

broadening its offerings and increasing profitability. This approach is typical of the **Cheaper, Better, Faster** model, where Revolut first gained traction by focusing on a single, cost-effective solution, then expanded to create a more comprehensive financial platform. For **customers**, this translated into significantly lower fees, greater convenience, and a simplified, mobile-first experience.

Incumbents were impacted as Revolut's pricing structure put pressure on traditional banks, pushing them to lower their fees, invest in digital platforms, and improve their offerings to remain competitive. This disruptive effect reshaped customer expectations and set new standards for cost, convenience, and accessibility in the financial services sector, establishing Revolut as a one of the leaders in the Fintech space.

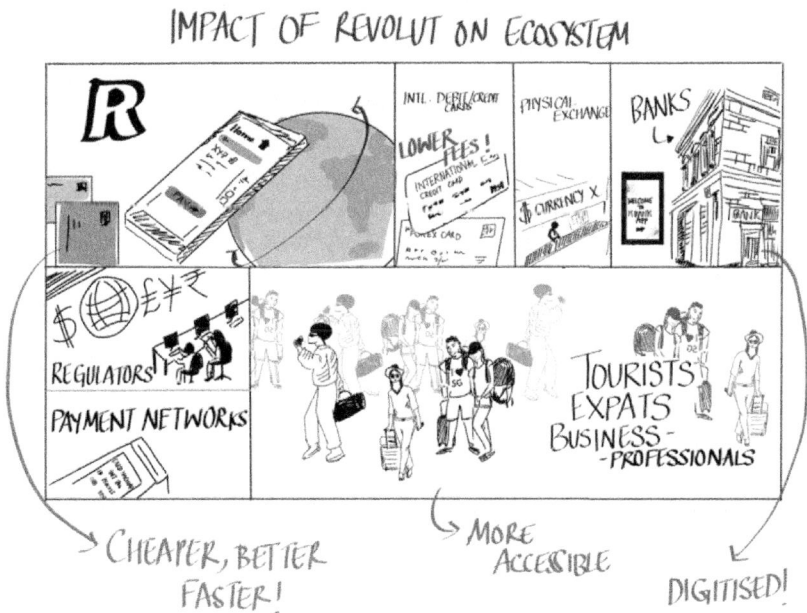

IMPACT OF REVOLUT ON ECOSYSTEM

141

II. Bitcoin: a Different vision of finance

Bitcoin was introduced in 2009 with the release of a white paper by the mysterious Satoshi Nakamoto, outlining a vision for a decentralised digital currency that would operate independently of governments and financial institutions. The goal was ambitious: to create a peer-to-peer electronic cash system that could bypass traditional banks entirely. This new approach to money marked Bitcoin as a perfect example of the **Different (D)** model, aiming to create a revolutionary alternative rather than competing directly within the existing financial ecosystem.

Bitcoin's growth trajectory has been both impressive and unpredictable. Initially, it attracted a niche group of early adopters who were captivated by its potential to disrupt the status quo. Over time, however, Bitcoin's influence has expanded far beyond this initial community, reshaping financial markets and regulatory landscapes across the globe. Today, Bitcoin is part of a **$2 trillion cryptocurrency market**, with an estimated **500 million users worldwide**. Its impact is so profound that nearly every regulator around the world is now involved in some aspect of the cryptocurrency space — whether through establishing regulations, exploring blockchain's applications in Central Bank Digital Currencies (CBDCs), or examining implications for anti-money laundering and financial stability.

However, as with many Different innovations, Bitcoin's evolution has been challenging to predict. Who could have anticipated that Nakamoto's white paper would not only inspire a digital currency but also lead to a wide array of uses, from speculative trading and a store of value (often called "digital gold") to the development of an entire Decentralised Finance (DeFi) ecosystem? Paradoxically, Bitcoin has even sparked innovation among the very institutions it aimed to bypass, as central banks and traditional banks explore blockchain and digital currency applications. This trajectory illustrates the hallmark of Different innovations: while they can be hugely impactful, their specific outcomes are often unexpected and complex.

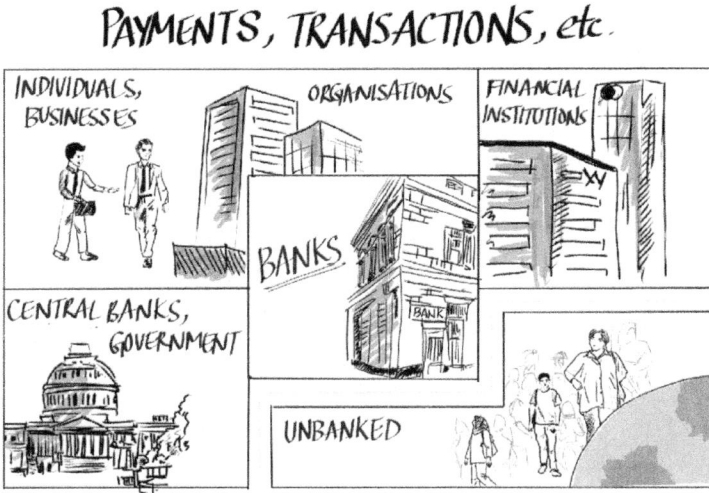

PAYMENTS, TRANSACTIONS, etc.

Bitcoin perfectly reflects the dynamics of the Different model — highly disruptive and widely influential, yet fundamentally unpredictable in its pathways and outcomes. Its impact has reverberated across finance, technology, and regulation, making it one of the most transformative and enigmatic innovations of the 21st century.

Let's explore Bitcoin's impact using the **EDGE** framework.

EDGE Analysis of Bitcoin

1. Existing Ecosystem

E D G E

- **Customers**: Prior to Bitcoin, customers relied on traditional financial institutions — banks, credit card companies, and money transfer services — for all forms of transactions, from everyday payments to international remittances. These services required trust in centralised entities to manage transactions and secure funds, while also charging fees and enforcing regulatory compliance.

- **Products/Services**: The existing system was fiat currencies such as the US dollar or Euro, managed by central banks, and supported by established institutions such as banks. They controlled money creation and distribution, as well as the infrastructure that facilitated financial transactions.

- **Incumbents**: Major incumbents included central banks, banks, credit card companies, and in general actors of financial services. These entities maintained a high degree of control over financial transactions, as part of a highly regulated environment.

- **Other Stakeholders**: since everybody is involved in money, other stakeholders were numerous, from businesses, merchants, investors to borrowers. Bitcoin's model was potentially a financial alternative that could operate outside the established systems on which these stakeholders rely.

2. Disruptor (New Entrant)

E D G E

- **Why**: Bitcoin was a revolutionary alternative to the existing payment system. Its creator, Satoshi Nakamoto, envisioned a new world of **decentralised finance** — one in which individuals could transact directly, without intermediaries or the oversight of traditional institutions. The goal was to establish a system based on the **Blockchain**, a technology that would enable trustless, transparent transactions, free from centralised control.

- **What**: At its core, Bitcoin is a digital asset that operates on a **decentralised, public ledger** (the Blockchain). The Blockchain allows Bitcoin to be a peer-to-peer currency, where transactions are verified through cryptographic proof rather than trusted third parties. This decentralisation was meant to remove the need for banks, empowering users to control their own assets and transfer value without institutional intervention.

- **How**: Bitcoin's open-source nature enabled anyone to participate in the network, either by running nodes to verify transactions or by mining to secure the network and mint new Bitcoin. This setup created a global network free from geographical or regulatory limitations. Bitcoin's design inherently challenged the existing financial order, proposing a world in which users controlled their own money and financial transactions could not be censored by any central authority.

3. Game Plan (Dynamics)

- **Disruptor Push**: Bitcoin was championed by a community of technologists, libertarians, and financial visionaries who believed in decentralisation, transparency, and individual sovereignty over wealth. Initially, Bitcoin advocates promoted it as a means to create a global financial system independent of banks and government control. Some envisioned it as "digital gold" — a hedge against inflation, resistant to manipulation and censorship. Through grassroots efforts, forums, and meetups, early adopters spread the word, contributing to the currency's growth and expanding awareness of Blockchain technology.

- **Customer Pull**: Bitcoin's first adopters were often ideologically aligned with its vision of financial freedom and autonomy. Over time, as more people became interested in the asset for its potential as a store of value and its ability to bypass traditional financial systems, its appeal broadened. The rise of exchanges and wallets made it easier to buy and store Bitcoin, attracting traders, speculators, and, eventually, institutional investors who began to see it as a legitimate asset class.

- **Incumbent Initial Pushback**: At first, most financial institutions dismissed Bitcoin as a fringe experiment. However, as its market capitalisation grew and its ecosystem developed, traditional financial institutions and regulators began to take notice. Some banks started exploring the underlying Blockchain technology, recognising its potential for secure, efficient record-keeping. Regulatory bodies took steps to classify, tax, or even ban Bitcoin in certain jurisdictions, citing concerns over its use in illicit activities and the risks it posed to monetary control. In a second stage however, financial institutions started to explore how Blockchain technology could streamline their operations, for example in tokenisation. And Central Banks started to test the Blockchain technology for **Central Bank Digital Currencies (CBDCs)**.

- **Other stakeholders**: While Bitcoin garnered some high-profile supporters — like Elon Musk's Tesla which invested $1.5 billion, or MicroStrategy, which invested $1 billion, the broader response from businesses was relatively reserved. Many stakeholders, from merchants to borrowers and traditional investors, were cautious, often viewing

Bitcoin as too volatile or unregulated for mainstream adoption. Some fund managers however launched Bitcoin funds and ETFs to capitalise on the retail interest of the cryptocurrency.

4. End Result (Impact)

- **Customers**: Bitcoin provided users with a way to store and transfer value outside the traditional financial system. It introduced the concept of digital ownership that didn't require reliance on banks or governments, allowing customers to engage in borderless transactions. However, Bitcoin's value proposition eventually evolved; instead of being primarily a peer-to-peer currency, it became a store of value as well as a speculative asset for investors.

- **Products**: Beyond Bitcoin itself, the underlying **Blockchain** technology sparked a wave of innovation, leading to the creation of **Decentralised Finance (DeFi)** applications that aim to provide traditional financial services — such as lending, borrowing, and trading — without intermediaries. Blockchain's influence extended far beyond Bitcoin, as financial institutions began to explore tokenisation and digital assets. This shift also inspired central banks to investigate **Central Bank Digital Currencies (CBDCs)** as they sought to modernise their own currencies. Ironically, this broader adoption by centralised entities diverged significantly from Bitcoin's original vision of decentralised, peer-to-peer finance, showing just how unpredictable the trajectory of **Different** innovations can be.

- **Incumbents**: Traditional financial institutions were initially sceptical of Bitcoin, seeing it as a fringe technology with limited practical applications or worse, an instrument

147

for money laundering. However, as its popularity grew and Blockchain technology gained recognition, banks and other financial players began exploring how this technology could benefit their operations. Many large banks now experiment with private blockchains for record-keeping and transaction security, while others are looking at tokenisation for digital assets. Governments and regulatory bodies were initially resistant to Bitcoin's promise of decentralised, anonymous transactions, as they feared its potential to enable money laundering and financial crime. Over time, however, governments began exploring ways to incorporate digital assets within existing regulatory frameworks, while some countries (such as El Salvador) went as far as to adopt Bitcoin as legal tender. Bitcoin also sparked interest in **Central Bank Digital Currencies (CBDCs)**, as governments sought to create digital currencies that could offer some of Bitcoin's technological advantages without sacrificing centralised control. This response highlighted a paradox: Bitcoin's original goal of challenging centralised power led to a wave of interest in Blockchain by the very institutions it aimed to circumvent.

- **Other Stakeholders**: The broader impact of Bitcoin on traditional stakeholders — such as businesses, merchants, investors, and borrowers — has been relatively muted due to volatility and regulatory concerns. However, Bitcoin and blockchain technology have introduced a new class of stakeholders, including exchanges like Coinbase and Binance, technology companies such as Ripple or R3, or analytics such as Chainalysis.

E EXISTING ECOSYSTEM	D DISRUPTOR	G GAME PLAN	E END RESULT
CUSTOMER INDIVIDUAL TRADERS, GENERAL PEOPLE	BITCOIN	DISRUPTOR PUSH ↳ DIGITAL GOLD → CHAMPIONED BY VISIONARIES → HEDGE	😊 CUSTOMERS. → DIGITAL OWNERSHIP
PRODUCT MONEY • STORE OF VALUE	DECENTRALISED FINANCE	CUSTOMER PULL → FINANCIAL AUTONOMY → STORE OF VALUE → BYPASS TRADFI	😊 PRODUCT. → DEFI → TOKENISATION ... CBDCs ?
INCUMBENT BANKS CREDIT CARD COMPANY CENTRAL BANKS REGULATORS	BLOCKCHAIN TECHNOLOGY DIGITAL ASSETS	INCUMBENT PUSH-BACK → DISMISSAL AS EXPERIMENT → TENTATIVE EXPLORATION → REGULATORS →TAX, CLASSIFY, BAN	😐 INCUMBENTS → INITIAL SKEPTICISM → BROADER ADOPTION BY FIs
OTHER STAKEHOLDERS BUSINESSES & MERCHANTS		STAKEHOLDER REACTION → MUTED	😊 GOVERNMENTS →CBDCs 😐 REGULATORS

How Bitcoin Followed the Different Pattern

Bitcoin is a prime example of **Different** innovation. It was launched with a vision not just to improve existing financial services but to create a radically new financial ecosystem that would operate outside the influence of central banks and traditional financial institutions. Bitcoin's decentralised nature allowed individuals to engage in peer-to-peer transactions without relying on any central authority, inspired by the revolutionary potential of **Blockchain** technology. The original vision was to establish a new financial system that was transparent, trustless, and censorship-resistant, giving people full control over their assets.

However, the actual impact of Bitcoin has been quite different from its original vision. Rather than transforming everyday transactions, Bitcoin's primary use has evolved into that of a store of value — a form of "digital gold" — that appeals to investors as a hedge against inflation and economic instability. Its underlying technology, Blockchain, has spawned a much broader ecosystem, including **Decentralised Finance (DeFi)** and **Central Bank Digital Currencies (CBDCs)**, both of which use Blockchain in ways that reflect a mix of decentralised and centralised control. Banks and financial institutions have also adopted Blockchain for tasks like tokenisation, digital asset management, and secure record-keeping, in direct contrast to Bitcoin's original aim of decentralised empowerment.

The trajectory of Bitcoin demonstrates how **Different** innovations can have unpredictable impacts. While its initial vision was to establish a purely decentralised financial system, the resulting influence has been far more complex, contributing to a mix of decentralised and centralised solutions. As Bitcoin has shown, **Different** innovations often lead to unexpected outcomes and create new industries, technologies, and regulatory frameworks that diverge from the original intent. This inherent unpredictability makes it challenging to foresee how such innovations will evolve and what lasting impacts they will have on established systems.

III. Stripe: enhancing small businesses for digital commerce

Founded in 2010, Stripe started with a clear objective: to make online payments accessible and easy for small businesses and developers. Unlike traditional payment processors, Stripe focused on a developer-first approach, offering a streamlined API that allowed small and medium-sized enterprises (SMEs) to integrate digital payments into their platforms with minimal hassle. Stripe's role as an Enhancer perfectly aligns with the **Enhancing (E)** model, aiming to help businesses by making complex processes accessible and user-friendly.

Stripe's growth has been remarkable. Starting as a simple payments solution, it rapidly evolved into a comprehensive financial platform. Today, Stripe supports **over 3 million websites** and processes more than **$1 trillion in payments annually**. By expanding its offerings to include products like Stripe Atlas (for business incorporation), Stripe Connect (for marketplace payments), and Stripe Billing (for subscription management), Stripe has rebundled financial services in a way that provides SMEs with a complete toolkit for digital operations. This breadth of services has made Stripe an invaluable asset for businesses looking to scale, reach global customers, and manage their finances efficiently in a digital-first world.

The success of Stripe shows that **Enhancing** innovations can be very significant: its impact has been substantial, reshaping how businesses of all sizes approach digital payments and e-commerce. Stripe raised the bar for payment processing by setting new standards for ease of integration, transparency, and flexibility. This influence has been so pervasive that traditional banks and payment processors have had to either partner with Stripe or adapt their own models to keep up with the demand for developer-friendly solutions.

Stripe's trajectory aligns well with the expectations of the Enhancing model. By empowering SMEs with tools they previously lacked, it has played a crucial role in expanding digital commerce accessibility. Stripe's emphasis on seamless integration and developer-focused design has not only transformed the digital payment landscape but has also driven broader innovations within the Fintech ecosystem. In doing so, Stripe has established itself as an indispensable enabler of e-commerce, showing how Enhancing innovations can also drive profound change.

EDGE Analysis of Stripe

E   D   G   E

1. Existing Ecosystem

E   D   G   E

- **Customers**: Before Stripe, **the customers of SMEs** often had to engage with these businesses offline because many SMEs couldn't easily accept online payments. Traditional payment solutions were complex and costly for SMEs, meaning their customers lacked a straightforward way to make digital transactions. This limited customer access to SME products and services online, forcing them to rely on in-person transactions or other inconvenient payment methods.

- **Products/Services**: Traditional payment solutions for online transactions were tailored for larger enterprises, with services provided by banks and specialised payment processors. These solutions included lengthy onboarding, hardware integrations, and complex compliance requirements — elements that were particularly challenging for smaller businesses without dedicated financial or technical support. This left many SMEs without practical options for digital payment integration, limiting their ability to compete effectively in the online market.

- **Incumbents**: In this context, **SMEs were the incumbents** challenged by the difficulty of integrating modern digital payment systems. Although they already served a customer base, their ability to operate digitally was constrained by traditional financial processes. The existing payment infrastructure prioritised larger businesses equipped to handle the associated costs, onboarding complexity, and compliance requirements, making it challenging for SMEs to serve their end customers with convenient digital payment options.

- **Other Stakeholders**: Credit card networks (such as Visa and Mastercard), financial regulators, and banks were key players in the ecosystem. These stakeholders influenced the regulatory framework and infrastructure on which payment processing relied, often geared towards established businesses with access to financial expertise.

2. Disruptor (New Entrant)

- **Why**: Stripe entered the market to remove the friction and barriers that SMEs faced in establishing an online presence and accepting digital payments. The founders, Patrick and John Collison, saw an opportunity to provide an accessible, easy-to-integrate payment processing solution specifically designed to empower small businesses and startups, allowing them to focus on growth rather than grappling with complex payment systems.

- **What**: Stripe's primary offering was a simple, developer-friendly API that allowed businesses to integrate digital payments into their websites or apps with minimal setup and cost. This API-focused solution enabled businesses to quickly start accepting payments without needing a complicated merchant account setup or hardware integration, making online payment capabilities accessible to a broader audience.

- **How**: Stripe designed a platform that allowed businesses to integrate payments seamlessly by copying a few lines of code, transforming the payment experience from a costly, complex process to a simple, scalable solution. By focusing on user-friendly documentation, straightforward onboarding, and transparent pricing, Stripe made digital payment processing accessible for SMEs that previously struggled to offer this capability.

3. Game Plan (Dynamics)

E   D   G   E

- **Disruptor Push**: Stripe's strategy was to build a platform that removed traditional barriers to digital payments for SMEs, helping them to offer their customers seamless online payment options. By taking a developer-first approach, Stripe enabled SMEs, startups, and solo entrepreneurs to integrate payment processing without the need for complex systems or direct relationships with banks. As Stripe grew, it added features like fraud prevention, billing, and subscription management, allowing SMEs to scale their digital operations efficiently and meet the growing expectations of their customers.

- **Customer Pull**: Stripe's end customers — the customers of SMEs — were drawn to SMEs that could now offer straightforward, reliable online payment options. This demand encouraged more SMEs to adopt Stripe, seeing it as a user-friendly and flexible payment solution that met both operational needs and customer expectations. Stripe's transparent pricing and contract-free setup made it particularly appealing to SMEs eager to serve digital-first customers.

- **Incumbent Pull**: SMEs themselves saw Stripe as an opportunity to overcome the limitations of traditional payment systems. By adopting Stripe, SMEs could provide digital payment options that previously were too complex or costly to manage. Stripe's technology enabled these businesses to enhance their offerings, reach a wider customer base, and compete effectively in the online marketplace. This broad adoption by SMEs fueled Stripe's growth and helped shift the payment landscape toward accessible, developer-friendly solutions..

- **Other Stakeholder Reactions**: Initially, traditional banks were largely indifferent to Stripe, as it targeted a niche market of SMEs that didn't represent a significant portion of their business. However, Stripe's rapid success and expansion have since highlighted a significant missed opportunity. Banks have realised the value Stripe brought to the SME market and beyond, with some, like Goldman Sachs, choosing to partner with Stripe to offer additional services to Stripe's growing customer base. For regulators, the widespread adoption of digital payments by SMEs presented potential concerns, such as ensuring compliance with Know Your Customer (KYC) requirements and anti-money laundering laws. However, despite the increase in digital payment activity, Stripe's adherence to regulatory standards has helped maintain compliance within this expanded ecosystem, keeping regulatory issues manageable thus far.

4. End Result (Impact)

- **Customers**: With Stripe's innovations, customers now expect all businesses — whether large corporations or small SMEs — to accept digital payments. This shift has raised service expectations across the board, as consumers increasingly anticipate seamless, secure online payment options from any business, regardless of size. Stripe's accessible solution has contributed to setting this new standard for digital payment convenience and reliability.

- **Products**: Stripe began as a simple payment API but has evolved into a fully embedded payment solution for e-commerce. Now, Stripe has **rebundled** and provides a comprehensive suite of products that includes subscription management, multi-currency support, cryptocurrency payments, and fraud management. By rebundling these services, Stripe has created an integrated platform that addresses a wide range of financial needs, making digital payment solutions a core component of e-commerce functionality.

- **Incumbents**: Stripe's impact on SMEs, the incumbents in this space, has been transformative. By providing a user-friendly, cost-effective solution for digital payments, Stripe has enabled even small businesses to process payments internationally and with far greater speed than before. This empowerment allows SMEs to serve a global customer base and compete more effectively with larger businesses.

- **Other Stakeholders**: Among other stakeholders, large banks have experienced significant impacts. Traditionally, banks provided many of the payment processing systems that Stripe now handles, and while SMEs were not historically a major revenue source, Stripe's growing appeal to larger clients has resulted in opportunity costs for banks. The financial data Stripe accumulates has become a valuable resource, one that banks have lost direct access to as they ceded this space. Meanwhile, credit card networks like Visa and Mastercard have benefitted from increased transaction volume, as Stripe's expansion has facilitated more frequent and accessible digital payments across a wider range of businesses.

E	D	G	E
EXISTING ECOSYSTEM	DISRUPTOR	GAME PLAN	END RESULT
CUSTOMER		DISRUPTOR PUSH	☺ CUSTOMERS
CUSTOMERS WHO BUY FROM SMEs ONLINE		· DEVELOPER-FIRST APPROACH · TARGETED SMEs, START-UPS, ETC	→ HIGHER CUSTOMER EXPECTATIONS
PRODUCT	STRIPE	CUSTOMER PULL	☺ PRODUCT
DIGITAL PAYMENTS	·ONLINE + DIGITAL PAYMENTS	→ ACCESS MORE SHOP ONLINE → BETTER UX	·EXPANDED FROM APIs TO INTEGRATED FINANCIAL TOOLKIT FOR ORGS.
INCUMBENT	INTEGRATED API	INCUMBENT PULL	☺ INCUMBENTS
SMEs (WHO FOUND IT HARD TO RECEIVE ONLINE PAYMENTS)		· SIMPLICITY · EASE-OF-USE · LOW STARTUP TIME	·ENABLED NEW WAVE OF BUSINESSES ·EXPAND MARKET
OTHER STAKEHOLDERS		STAKEHOLDER REACTION	☺ INDUSTRY's STANDARDS ↑
CREDIT-CARD NETWORKS BANKS, FINANCIAL REGULATORS		→ LITTLE REACTION INITIALLY	☹ OTHER FIs

How Stripe Followed the Enhancing Pattern

Stripe illustrates the **Enhancing** innovation pattern by focusing on tools that improve accessibility, productivity, and efficiency for SMEs, allowing them to enter the digital marketplace with minimal friction. Unlike disruptors that aim to replace existing products or create something entirely novel, Stripe sought to empower businesses by providing them with an easy-to-use platform for payment processing.

This approach enabled companies to set up digital payments quickly, improve cash flow, and focus on growing their business rather than navigating complex financial systems. By removing technical and financial barriers, Stripe helped businesses — from startups to established SMEs — boost their productivity and deliver better services to their customers.

Stripe's initial product strategy followed an **unbundling** approach, starting with a single, developer-friendly API for payments. As the platform grew and gained traction, it **rebundled** by adding complementary services, such as fraud prevention, invoicing, and subscription management, creating a comprehensive toolkit for digital business operations. This rebundling allowed Stripe to cater to a broader range of business needs and establish itself as a versatile partner for SMEs.

For **Incumbents**, Stripe's tools enhanced their ability to compete in the digital economy. Many SMEs previously found it difficult or impossible to accept payments online due to the costs and complexities involved. Stripe made this accessible, allowing small businesses to expand their market reach and serve a global audience.

Overall, Stripe exemplifies the type of **Enhancing** innovation that helps existing players to deliver cheaper, better and faster products themselves.

Part IV:

The Three Trends Shaping AI's Impact on Jobs

Mass displacement, supercharged professionals, and creative disruptors

How will AI impact me?

I love learning from others. I also love sharing what I've learnt. We often think of learning as a student listening to a professor or an employee in front of a screen. But structured learning is only 10% of how we build our knowledge. The remaining 90% comes from our own experiences, especially interactions with others.

I learn from many people, often in the context of my industry — from central banks to regulators, tech companies, and startups. More than 1,000 experts teach on CFTE's platform, and while this benefits the community, for me, it's a dream come true!

Whenever I meet someone, I always enjoy talking about AI and Fintech. But until very recently, most people outside the industry were not that interested — except to ask if they should buy Bitcoin!

This has changed drastically in the past few years.

Today, I have lengthy discussions with people from all walks of life who have strong views on AI. I remember a very smart hotel receptionist in Liverpool who, despite knowing AI well, was deeply pessimistic about his future. He shared about his friend working in events in London, whose job was increasingly threatened by AI. An immigration officer at the Zurich airport noticed my AI pin and wondered if the growing presence of ePassport gates was truly a step forward. At dinner parties, conversations often revolve around AI and how to prepare our children for its impact, right after discussing food!

AI has become personal, as we explored in the previous chapter. Since jobs are such an important part of our identity and well-being, questions about AI's effect on work have become the most pressing. Just look at the questions people search for on Google: we all want to know how AI will impact our jobs.

Q   Will AI| ✕   🎤   📷

Q   will ai **take over the world**

Q   will ai **replace programmers**

Q   will ai **take my job**

Q   will ai **replace accountants**

Q   will ai **take over jobs**

Q   will ai **replace teachers**

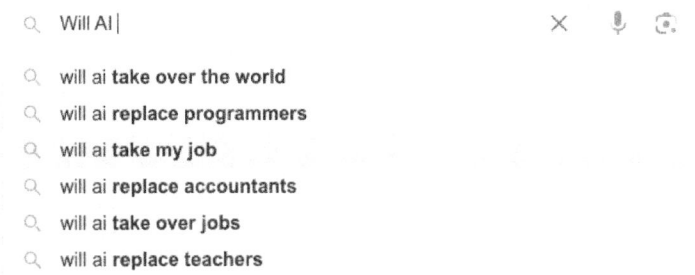

Or take the findings from ADP's 2024 Global Workforce View survey as another example. It showed that:

- 85% of employees believe AI will impact their jobs within the next 2 to 3 years.
- Half think AI will help with some or many of their tasks.
- Half think AI will replace some or many of their tasks.

These statistics reflect how deeply AI has entered our professional lives. Just one year after ChatGPT's release, almost everyone had an opinion on how AI will change their work. The divide is clear: half are optimistic, half are worried.

What makes AI's impact so personal is that it challenges not just the future of work, but our own roles, skills, and sense of identity. Many conversations about AI are emotional rather than logical, and understandably so — our jobs are tied to how we define ourselves.

In this chapter, we'll set aside emotion and intuition and take a structured approach to understanding AI's impact on jobs. Through the lens of the **CDE Innovation Prism**, we'll identify three major trends already taking shape: **mass displacement**, **supercharged professionals**, and **creative disruptors**.

Understanding these trends allows us to move from emotional reactions to thoughtful predictions. So, join me as we explore how AI will transform jobs using the framework of

Cheaper/Better/Faster, **Different**, and **Enhancing** innovations.

What Do We Mean by "AI's Impact on Jobs"?

When people ask how AI will impact jobs, they're often grappling with personal questions about their futures — questions filled with both excitement and anxiety. AI promises to revolutionise industries by taking over mundane, repetitive tasks, freeing up time for higher-value work. But it also raises fears of widespread job displacement.

So what are we really asking?

Key Questions People Are Asking

In my discussions around the world, I find that there are 4 recurring topics which people are mostly interested in:

1. **Will my job be replaced?** This is the most immediate concern. As AI gets better at "human" skills, many worry that their jobs will be eliminated, including those in white collar jobs previously thought as safe. The real question is: which jobs are actually at risk?
2. **Will my job be enhanced?** Some wonder whether AI will augment their work rather than replace it, acting as a tool to improve productivity and allow them to focus on higher-level tasks.
3. **Will new jobs be created?** Much like previous technological revolutions, AI is expected to create entirely new roles that don't exist yet. What new roles will AI bring, and who will fill them?
4. **What skills will I need?** As AI reshapes industries, workers are wondering which skills they should develop to stay relevant. Jobs requiring creativity, emotional intelligence, and complex decision-making seem less likely to be automated — but what specific skills will ensure employability?

162

The Human-Centric Perspective

These questions are very personal. They touch on how we define ourselves through our work and what value we bring to the workforce. Whether you're on the frontline or a policymaker, the debate around AI and jobs circles back to a single concern: **What happens to me?**

Naturally, these questions are emotionally charged. When technology like AI threatens our roles, it's only human to feel uncertain. But while these are important questions, we need a more structured way to approach them.

The Shift in Perspective: Viewing AI as the Disruptor

Trying to predict the future of specific jobs is incredibly complex because each role is a mix of tasks — some repetitive, others creative — and every industry adopts AI at a different pace. This complexity often makes it feel like we're focusing on a single piece of a massive puzzle, unable to see the bigger picture.

The real challenge in answering these questions isn't just the variability of jobs — it's the **perspective** we're using. We tend to look at this issue through the eyes of the **incumbent** — how workers and companies will respond to disruption. But that doesn't always help us predict the broader changes that occur.

It's like viewing the rise of Amazon solely from the perspective of bookshops, rather than considering what Jeff Bezos might do to redefine retail. Similarly, when social media platforms like Facebook emerged, seeing it from the perspective of newspapers could explain their immediate decline — but not the massive new industries that followed, like digital marketing or influencer careers.

This brings us to AI. To truly understand its impact on jobs, we need to shift our perspective and look at AI as the **disruptor**. What opportunities do AI companies see? Where can AI outperform humans by being Cheaper, Better, or Faster? And what new roles might emerge as a result of AI's capabilities?

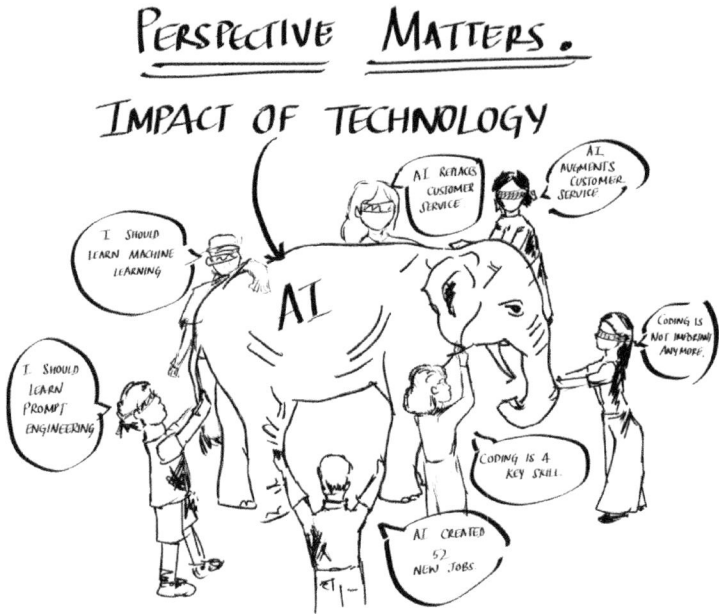

This is where the **CDE Innovation Prism** becomes very useful. Instead of focusing solely on how workers or companies will react, we use the framework to shift our perspective to **AI as the innovation driver**. By adopting this broader viewpoint, we can anticipate how AI will impact jobs and industries.

Let's explore these trends in detail, using the CDE Prism to guide us in understanding how AI will reshape the world of work.

Understanding AI's Impact Through the Lens of Innovation Dynamics

Introduction to AI as a Disruptor: The Innovation Lens

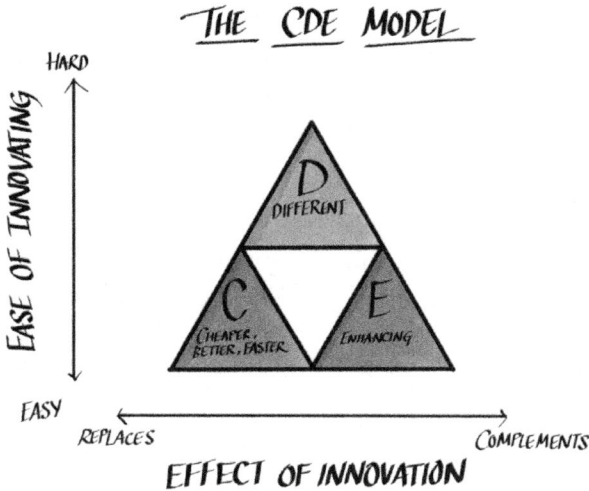

In **Chapter 2**, we saw how previous technological disruptions often had **collateral effects** on jobs. For example, the rise of e-commerce led to bookstore closures, but the job losses were indirect consequences of Amazon's dominance, rather than the immediate target of the innovation. Similarly, when Facebook transformed communication, it led to the creation of entirely new jobs (digital marketers, social media managers, influencers), yet this was a by-product of the platform's larger social ecosystem.

Innovations like the steam engine or the Internet reshaped tools, processes, and ecosystems — factories were reorganised, supply chains were transformed. Workers had to adapt to new systems or tools, but the focus remained on restructuring workflows and improving efficiency.

AI, however, is **different**. Its impact on jobs is **direct**, because AI replicates human tasks and skills themselves. Rather than just introducing new systems or tools, AI can now take over specific tasks, such as automating customer service inquiries or generating detailed reports. It's no longer about changing how work is organised, but about directly influencing the **work itself**. AI's ability to automate, augment, and even create new functions means the **impact on jobs is immediate** and goes straight to the core of what many workers do on a daily basis.

In other words, when applying the EDGE Canvas to AI as the disruptive innovation, **humans themselves become the Incumbents**. The roles, tasks, and skills traditionally performed by people are directly impacted by AI's ability to replicate or enhance those functions.

The EDGE Canvas: Mapping AI's Impact on Jobs

To understand AI's impact on jobs, we will consider AI as a new entrant within an established ecosystem — potentially as broad as the economy itself, with all its diverse sectors, companies, employers, and employees. Each component of this ecosystem — from specific industries to the interactions between employers and their workforce — adds layers of complexity to AI's influence on work.

AI, as the disruptor, brings a transformative set of capabilities and priorities that transforms and reshape this ecosystem. To gain clearer insights into how AI is reshaping jobs within this framework, we will apply the **EDGE Canvas** and explore the three approaches of the **CDE Prism** (Cheaper/Better/Faster, Different, and Enhancing).

1. Existing Ecosystem

- **Customer**: In this context, the customer is **an employer or a company that needs jobs to be done** — whether it's a large corporation, a tech startup, or even a freelance client. These customers traditionally rely on human labour to perform specific tasks, such as answering customer inquiries, analysing data, or driving cars.
- **Product**: The product here is not a physical good or service — it is the **job itself**. Each task that human workers perform — whether it's writing reports, managing customer service, or making strategic decisions — constitutes the product. These jobs, in a sense, are what companies "purchase" to keep their operations running.
- **Incumbent**: The incumbents in this framework are **human workers** — employees, consultants, freelancers, or any individual whose work contributes to fulfilling these job tasks. These workers have developed specific skill sets to meet the demands of the job and, until now, have been essential to the functioning of industries.

2. Disruptor

- **Disruptor**: The disruptor is **AI itself** — specifically the companies and technologies that provide AI-driven solutions, such as chatbots, machine learning algorithms, or robotic process automation (RPA). They can either compete or collaborate with the Incumbent, or create totally new sectors.

A Deeper Dive into the EDGE Canvas

This step-by-step application of the EDGE Canvas reveals the **direct dynamic** of AI's impact on jobs. Let's break it down in more detail:

- **Customer**: Employers are constantly seeking efficiency, profitability, and scalability. For these employers, AI could be seen as an alternative workforce, that could either complement or sometimes replace their human workforce. When previous Operating Models relied on 3 distinct areas (PPT: People, Process, Technology), the distinction becomes more blurry in an AI world.

- **Product**: The "product" has fundamentally changed. While traditionally companies "purchased" human time and effort, AI now presents an alternative, where the "job" can be performed by software. Whether it's data analysis, content creation, or customer service, the "product" has evolved from human labour to machine-driven output.

- **Incumbent**: The human worker sees a new entrant in the world of work. AI could be seen either as a new tool, sometimes a new colleague, or even a new competitor. This makes the impact of AI on jobs **far more personal** than previous technological revolutions, and the dynamics for AI tend to be much more emotionally charged.

- **Disruptor**: The AI companies — like OpenAI, Google, or Microsoft — are the disruptors in this context. Their objective is to find good market opportunities for their even more powerful technologies, and they will usually follow any of the 3 approaches of the CDE Prism.

By using the **EDGE Canvas**, we can clearly see the direct impact of AI on jobs. Now that we've mapped out the dynamics, we're ready to explore how this disruption unfolds through the lens of the **CDE Innovation Prism**.

The Cheaper/Better/Faster Impact on Jobs

The first major trend we see with AI innovation is its drive to make tasks Cheaper/Better/Faster. This category of innovation focuses on efficiency and cost reduction — streamlining operations, improving accuracy, and replacing human labour where AI offers superior performance.

Defining Cheaper, Better, Faster AI: The Perspective of the AI Disruptor

When we talk about Cheaper, Better, Faster AI, we are talking about the classic strategy that any successful disruptor follows: identifying an existing product or service — in this case, jobs or activities performed by humans — and finding a way to do them more efficiently. This is no different from what Amazon did with books or Revolut with payments. The goal is to improve the speed, cost, and quality of existing work, but here the competition is not another company — it's human labour.

Cheaper, Better, Faster Than What?

Cheaper, Better, Faster AI is always measured against what already exists, and in this context, that means human workers. The AI provider aims to replace or augment human roles with algorithms and automated processes that are more efficient in terms of cost, speed, or accuracy.

Even if AI companies don't directly reference human workers, their comparisons in terms of cost, quality, or speed implicitly highlight the difference. For example, when an AI company advertises that "chatbots are more affordable than agents," "cut support costs by 27%," or "what used to take 19 days now takes 15 minutes," the underlying message is that AI solutions outperform the human incumbents in these roles.

From the AI provider's perspective, this is a standard approach to innovation, with the objective of finding a Product Market Fit. This means aligning what they offer with what the market needs, and for Cheaper, Better, Faster AI, this boils down to two factors:

1. **AI Capabilities:** The AI solution must be able to match or exceed human performance in the target job. This is why we often see AI starting in industries or roles that are routine, predictable, and data-intensive — tasks that AI can handle consistently and with fewer errors than humans.

2. **Market Size**: The target market must be large enough to make the disruption worthwhile. The most appealing targets are sectors that employ a high volume of workers in repetitive tasks, such as customer service, content moderation, or data entry.

Key Characteristics of Cheaper, Better, Faster AI

For the AI Disruptor to be interesting to the clients, it needs to offer a very strong value proposition by being significantly cheaper, better and/or faster than the incumbent.

Cheaper: A primary appeal of AI is its cost-saving potential. Unlike human labour, AI systems can operate continuously, without the costs of overtime pay, healthcare, or vacation time. Once in place, AI performs tasks at a fraction of the cost of human workers, allowing organisations to reduce their operating expenses significantly.

Better: AI can surpass human abilities in certain areas by handling tasks that humans find challenging or even impossible. AI can process and analyse enormous amounts of data far beyond what any person could manage, giving it a knowledge base that no single individual can rival. AI can speak dozens of languages, allowing them to serve diverse populations more effectively than a single language-based team. These capabilities enable AI to offer capabilities on a scale that can exceed human skills.

Faster: AI's speed advantage is transformative, as it can complete tasks that would take humans hours or even days in just seconds or minutes. For routine tasks AI can perform similarly to humans — like data processing or calculations — it's impossible for people to match AI's efficiency. Just as most of us can't outpace a calculator, humans can't compete with AI's processing speed, particularly when it comes to repetitive or computationally intensive tasks. This sheer speed enables AI to perform tasks at a rate that fundamentally changes the scale at which organisations can operate.

The Product-Market Fit of AI

For AI providers, achieving product-market fit means demonstrating that their technology can handle key functions in the workplace cheaper, better, and faster than humans. However, this isn't just about replacing one role with another; it's about positioning AI as a superior alternative in large, labour-intensive markets.

There are many areas that are currently being targeted by AI companies, for example:

- Customer service: AI chatbots can handle millions of queries simultaneously, with no downtime, across multiple languages, far exceeding human capabilities in cost and efficiency.

- Data entry: AI can automatically extract, sort, and categorise data from documents, saving hours of manual input while reducing human error.

- Manufacturing: Robots powered by AI can perform repetitive tasks such as assembly, welding, and packaging faster and with fewer mistakes than human workers.

These sectors represent massive markets where routine tasks dominate, making them ripe for disruption by Cheaper, Better, Faster AI. This is however just the start – there are tens of thousands of AI startups looking for product market fit.

The Push for Routine, Repeatable Processes

For AI providers, it's essential to focus on tasks that are routine, predictable, and repeatable. This is where AI excels. Whether it's responding to customer inquiries, approving loan applications, or even performing basic medical diagnostics, AI thrives in areas where processes are clear, well-defined, and data-driven.

This is why AI disruptors often unbundle a larger process into smaller, more manageable tasks that AI can perform. Once AI has proven its value in one area (such as automating customer service inquiries), it can rebundle by expanding into adjacent tasks (such as handling customer complaints, upselling, or generating insights from customer data).

This process of unbundling and rebundling ensures that AI providers establish strong product-market fit in one function before expanding into others, much like how Amazon started with books before becoming the "everything store."

What Does Cheaper/Better/Faster AI Look Like in Practice?

Cheaper/Better/Faster AI is about optimising processes to reduce costs, improve performance, and challenge human labour directly. From the perspective of AI providers, this innovation strategy identifies specific market opportunities where AI can outperform humans — whether by executing tasks faster, at a lower cost, or with improved accuracy. The disruptor's goal is to create a product that delivers superior results while matching two critical conditions: the AI must be capable enough to take on routine, scalable tasks, and the market must be large enough to justify the investment.

The most striking feature of Cheaper/Better/Faster AI is how **quickly** it's being adopted. Just two years ago, many of the examples we discuss here would have been seen as futuristic. Today, companies are already making sweeping changes, with AI displacing human workers at scale in ways that would have been impossible in 2022. Below are some real-world examples of this transformation, showing how companies are using AI to reshape their operations.

Klarna: Replacing Customer Service Agents with AI

Klarna, a global leader in Buy Now, Pay Later (BNPL) services, embraced AI to streamline its customer service operations. In 2023, Klarna's CEO announced the integration of ChatGPT Enterprise across its operations, including customer service, marketing, and legal departments. By 2024, Klarna had replaced over 700 customer service agents with AI chatbots, saving the company $40 million per year. These chatbots not only handled customer inquiries faster (reducing response time from 11 minutes to just 2 minutes) but also provided service in multiple languages, around the clock.

The human cost, however, was significant. **Klarna reduced its customer service workforce by 20%, displacing hundreds of human agents.** AI's ability to perform at speed, scale, and reduced costs makes it a compelling choice for businesses like Klarna, where customer service is a critical, yet routine, function.

Klarna will be studied as a case study later in the chapter.

TikTok: Cutting Content Moderation Jobs in Malaysia

In 2024, TikTok made headlines by cutting several hundred content moderation jobs in Malaysia, replacing many of these roles with AI-driven systems. Content moderation is essential for platforms like TikTok, which processes millions of videos daily. Previously, large teams of human moderators were responsible for flagging inappropriate content — a labour-intensive task that required monitoring videos around the clock.

By leveraging AI, TikTok significantly reduced its reliance on human moderators. AI systems now automatically scan videos, flag violations, and take immediate action, making content moderation faster and more scalable than ever before. The speed and consistency with which AI can analyse videos and enforce content guidelines proved to be faster, more cost-effective, and equally as reliable as human moderators.

Duolingo: Reducing Translators by 10%

In 2024, Duolingo, the popular language-learning app, cut its number of human translators by 10%, citing AI as the reason. Duolingo had traditionally relied on human translators to create new exercises and ensure language accuracy across its platforms. However, with advances in AI-driven translation models, the company found that AI could handle much of this work, particularly the repetitive tasks of translating routine exercises.

Duolingo continues to use human translators for more complex tasks, but AI now manages a large portion of the translation workload, enabling the company to scale its content creation faster and at a lower cost. As a result, Duolingo expanded into new languages more quickly, with fewer translators on staff.

The Appeal of Cheaper, Better, Faster

In all three examples, AI didn't just assist humans; it replaced a significant portion of the workforce. The quality of the tasks performed by AI — whether in customer service, content moderation, or translation — was comparable to, or even better than, what human workers were delivering. And the speed of AI's performance, combined with its scalability, is unmatched.

Just as we use AI tools like ChatGPT to draft emails or generate content, companies like Klarna, TikTok, and Duolingo are applying these tools on a much larger scale. The quality of interactions in customer service or the accuracy of analysing videos is not only comparable to humans but often superior. In terms of cost, the choice is obvious — while human employees cost thousands of dollars per month,

ChatGPT costs as little as $20 per month. Although the roles are not directly comparable, this significant cost difference explains why companies are increasingly adopting AI to replace human roles.

What This Means for Jobs

For human workers, the most immediate impact of Cheaper/Better/Faster AI is **job displacement**. Tasks that can be automated — especially those involving routine, predictable work — are prime targets for replacement by AI. In Klarna's case, customer service roles were automated; in TikTok's case, content moderation; and in Duolingo's case, translation tasks.

However, the broader implications of Cheaper/Better/Faster AI extend beyond job replacement. While many routine jobs will be displaced, we will also see hybrid roles emerging — where human workers manage or oversee AI processes. This opens up opportunities for reskilling and transitioning into roles that focus on AI oversight and interpretation. As AI continues to evolve, the line between automation and augmentation will blur, with some roles disappearing while others are transformed into AI-augmented jobs.

Next, we'll explore the dynamics driving this type of innovation and how these changes are reshaping industries and employment at a global scale.

The Dynamics of Cheaper, Better, Faster

AI companies driving the Cheaper, Better, Faster revolution in job markets are guided by a clear go-to-market strategy, starting with identifying key business opportunities. Their initial focus is on finding the intersection between where AI excels and where there is a large workforce — this provides a clear path for both economic and technological disruption.

- AI will target specific sectors first, where AI is performant and the market is big
- AI companies begin by targeting sectors where Generative AI and related technologies are particularly strong.

For example, customer service is a prime target because AI is highly capable of handling conversations, answering queries, resolving disputes, and interacting with customers in natural language. This is an area where Generative AI shines, as it can draw from vast datasets to provide human-like conversational capabilities at scale. Furthermore, customer service represents a large segment of the workforce, meaning there is substantial room for cost-saving and workforce replacement — two major incentives for businesses to adopt AI. AI companies see this sector as an immediate opportunity to showcase the potential of their technology.

However, customer service is just the beginning. AI companies have started to target many other verticals such as:

- Content creation: AI can now write, edit, and generate text, graphics, and videos, making roles like copywriting, marketing, and video production vulnerable.

- Translation and transcription services: AI's ability to process and understand multiple languages makes translation and transcription another key area where AI is taking over from humans.

- Administrative tasks: Routine tasks such as data entry, scheduling, and basic record-keeping are easily automated by AI, reducing the need for administrative personnel.

These areas are targeted because AI can perform the tasks more quickly, at a lower cost, and with fewer errors than human workers.

It starts with unbundling then continues with rebundling

Today, tens of thousands of startups operate in the AI space, and many are drawn to the Cheaper, Better, Faster model because it presents a low-hanging fruit. Not all AI companies focus on this model, but those that do often find it an accessible way to demonstrate clear, measurable value.

These AI companies will adopt an unbundling and rebundling strategy. In the unbundling phase, they will focus on narrow, high-impact areas where AI has a clear advantage, and where the market opportunity is large. For instance, customer service is an attractive market because Generative AI is capable of handling discussions and the sector employs a large number of workers, presenting a significant opportunity for cost reduction and automation.

By focusing on a specific function, AI companies can develop highly specialised tools that allow them to demonstrate the effectiveness of their technology. Once they establish credibility in one domain, they transition to the rebundling phase, expanding into adjacent areas. For example, an AI company initially focused on customer service may branch out to sales support, HR, marketing, or legal services. This rebundling allows them to leverage the trust they've built in one sector and create a broader suite of offerings, positioning themselves as comprehensive technology partners. By increasing their scope, they can gain a stronger foothold within organisations, gradually replacing or automating more human roles across multiple departments.

It's also important to note that while many of these AI startups may find early success, most will fail as part of the natural innovation process. The technology landscape is highly competitive, and for each successful AI disruptor, dozens of others will not reach significant scale. However, among those that succeed, a few may become dominant players. These "winner-takes-all" companies could grow to monopolise their respective markets, as they leverage AI's scalability to secure competitive advantages that are difficult for others to match.

It's also worth noting that these entrepreneurs are not aiming to displace human workers. Most of them are driven by a fascination with the technology itself and the market opportunities it presents. They view AI as a tool to enhance efficiency, streamline processes, and create value.

As I discussed in the Ethics in Fintech chapter of the Fintech Book, the issue with many tech entrepreneurs isn't that they're immoral — it's that they are often amoral. They focus on the potential of technology without necessarily considering the broader implications, such as job displacement. For them, the pursuit of Cheaper, Better, Faster innovations about driving technological progress — human workers are not really thought of as a collateral impact.

Employers will welcome AI

For many businesses, the economic case for adopting AI is compelling. AI systems offer substantial cost savings over human labour, which can be a critical factor for companies with tight budgets or aggressive growth targets. The cost difference between human workers and AI is staggering — often 99% cheaper for AI-based services. While AI is not always 100% the same as a human worker, the substantial cost difference is a powerful incentive for businesses to adopt AI tools.

For example, AI-powered customer service can reduce costs from tens of thousands of dollars per month for human staff to a few hundred dollars for AI systems, and translation services can drop from thousands of dollars to mere cents per word.

Service	Human Cost	AI Cost
Captioning	$120 per hour (human)	<$0.50 per hour (AI)
Translation services	$1,500 for 10,000 words (human)	$1-3 for 10,000 words (AI)
Customer service	~$4000 per month (US)	$100 per month (AI)

However, not all organisations will adopt AI at the same pace, and the adoption pattern usually follows the innovation lifecycle created by Everett Rogers. The early adopters of AI technologies are typically startups and tech companies, which tend to be more familiar with emerging technologies and less encumbered by legacy systems. Startups often face resource constraints, so they're motivated to find cost-effective solutions that can help them scale quickly. For these companies, adopting AI to replace dozens or even hundreds of roles allows them to reduce overhead, improve service efficiency, and allocate resources to other growth areas.

Larger organisations, on the other hand, are likely to be late adopters due to the complexity and scale of their existing operations. For these companies, adopting AI on a wide scale typically requires significant change management, including retraining employees and restructuring departments. Additionally, big companies may face more internal resistance, both from employees who feel threatened by the prospect of job displacement and from clients or stakeholders who might have ethical concerns about the impact of AI. Some institutional clients, for instance, may be wary of a company openly replacing human jobs with machines, and this could create hesitation for larger, more established organisations that

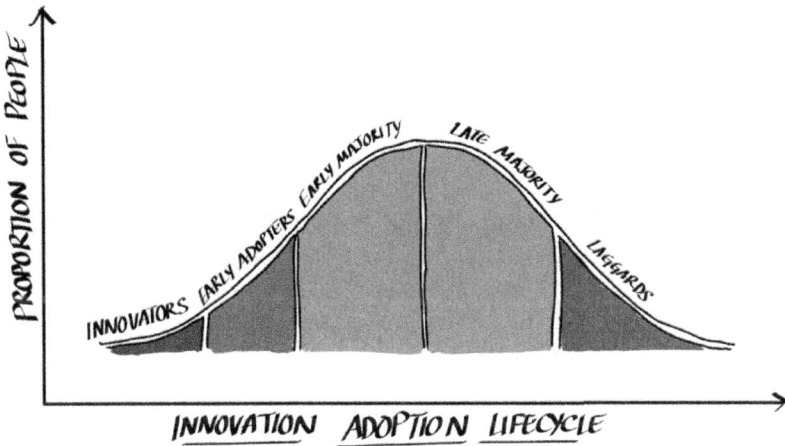

have reputations to maintain.

One exception, however, for large organisations, is in the area of outsourced activities. These tasks often follow well-defined workflows with clear rules and performance metrics, making them ideal for AI-driven solutions. Unlike other parts of the business, outsourced activities are typically less visible to the public and, therefore, carry lower reputational risk when automated. By applying AI to these processes, large organisations can achieve significant improvements in cost-efficiency, speed, and accuracy, allowing them to enhance service delivery without the same level of public or ethical scrutiny. This approach enables big companies to leverage AI competitively by focusing on "Cheaper, Better, Faster" outcomes in areas where disruption is minimal and operational gains are immediate. Please note that the AI implementation could be led either by the organisation or the outsourcer itself.

Thus, while the cost savings from AI adoption are highly appealing, particularly for early adopters, larger companies may move more slowly. They must consider not only the economic benefits but also the potential cultural and reputational impacts of replacing human roles with AI, balancing these against the efficiency and scalability gains AI promises. Nonetheless, as AI solutions continue to demonstrate substantial financial returns, even larger organisations are likely to follow suit, although on a more gradual trajectory.

Furthermore, employers don't just look at jobs as a one-to-one replacement. AI can unlock entirely new ways of doing things that are more efficient. For example, Mango, the fashion brand, has begun producing its marketing campaigns entirely with AI, eliminating the need for fashion models, photographers, and other creatives. In this case, AI-powered video editing tools were not only a cheaper and faster alternative but also a completely different approach to generating the same result — marketing campaigns — at a much lower cost and faster turnaround time. This illustrates how AI doesn't simply replace jobs in the same form, but redefines how companies can approach tasks and deliver outcomes.

Employees will try to push back

For employees, AI-driven transformations like those seen at Klarna present a daunting reality. Pushback among workers is common, as they recognise the direct threat AI poses to job security, wages, and long-term employability. While some sectors, such as the entertainment industry — evidenced by Hollywood writers going on strike — have organised to negotiate limits on AI's role, most employees lack such collective bargaining power. Many affected workers are facing reductions in wages, as is the case with professional translators, who have seen revenues fall by 40% due to AI competition.

This leaves employees with few options for effectively resisting AI's competition. Organised action may not be feasible for many sectors, meaning individual workers are often left to compete against a technology that's inherently scalable, cost-effective, and tireless. Beyond the financial strain, there's also a psychological impact: knowing that AI sets the new standard makes employees feel that their roles are being judged against an ideal that's extremely difficult to match. When displaced, they must also contend with the reality that their skills may no longer be valued by future employers, who might also prefer AI-driven solutions.

In essence, the employees' pushback is constrained not just by their lack of bargaining power but by the overwhelming economic incentives for companies to adopt AI. The traditional avenues of resistance — advocating for retraining or finding other roles within the company — are unlikely to be sufficient when entire job functions are replaced. This dynamic underscores a broader challenge: the push for Cheaper, Better, Faster innovations benefits all parties except the employees, who are the ones directly impacted by these AI-driven transformations.

Impact (End Result) of Cheaper, Better, Faster AI

The adoption of Cheaper, Better, Faster AI has profound consequences, with jobs being the most directly affected. The primary impact is mass job displacement, but the secondary impacts include job augmentation and the creation of new roles. After considering how AI impacts jobs, we can explore the effects on employers, products, and the broader ecosystem.

Impact on Jobs (Primary and Secondary)

1. **Primary Impact: Job Displacement at Scale**
- AI fundamentally reshapes industries by automating routine, repetitive tasks — especially those that involve data entry, customer service, and basic administrative work. This leads to large-scale job replacement, where entire departments or roles are eliminated.

- Real-world example: Klarna's implementation of AI chatbots displaced over 700 customer service agents, cutting costs dramatically while improving service efficiency. In cases like this, AI adoption leads to mass displacement in areas where tasks are predictable and repetitive.

2. **Secondary Impact: Job Augmentation**
- While AI replaces certain roles, it also augments existing jobs, enabling workers to focus on higher-level tasks that AI cannot perform. AI serves as a tool that enhances

productivity, assisting professionals in making quicker, more informed decisions or handling more complex tasks.

- Real-world example: Duolingo decreased the number of human translators by 10% and now uses AI for basic translation tasks. For the rest of the organisation, their model is "Human Experts + AI", where some tasks are mainly done by humans (such as curriculum design) while others are mainly AI (personalisation).

2. Secondary Impact: New Job Creation

- AI also paves the way for entirely new roles that didn't exist before. Just as previous technological revolutions created jobs like social media managers and app developers, AI is giving rise to positions such as AI trainers, AI ethicists, and AI-human collaboration specialists.

- Real-world example: The rise of AI in healthcare has introduced new roles like AI-assisted radiologists and robotic surgery specialists. These positions illustrate how AI can create opportunities in sectors where human expertise is irreplaceable.

2. Shifts in Job Complexity and Skill Requirements

- Many jobs will evolve into hybrid roles, where human workers collaborate with AI systems. Workers will need to retrain and reskill to remain relevant, with an emphasis on higher-order thinking, decision-making, and AI management. The workforce will transition toward roles that require problem-solving, creativity, and emotional intelligence — tasks AI struggles to replicate.

Impact on Employers

1. Cost Savings

- The most immediate benefit to employers is the significant reduction in labour costs. AI tools, which can work 24/7 without breaks, handle tasks far more efficiently and at a fraction of the cost of human labour. This cuts overhead costs dramatically and improves operational efficiency.

- For example, a human worker might cost a company $50,000 per year, whereas an AI system could provide similar results for just $1,000 per year, creating a direct financial incentive for businesses to adopt AI-driven solutions.

2. Increased Productivity and Output

- As AI takes over routine tasks, human employees are freed up to focus on higher-value activities, leading to an increase in productivity and overall output. AI augments human abilities, making workers more efficient, especially in complex tasks that require human judgement.

- Companies that integrate AI see an increase in revenue per employee, as fewer workers are needed to achieve the same (or even higher) levels of productivity.

2. Long-term Strategic Considerations

- In the short term, cost savings and productivity gains are apparent, but there are medium- to long-term risks in over-reliance on AI at the expense of human talent and innovation. Companies that neglect to balance AI with human creativity and skills may face cultural and strategic challenges down the line.

- For sustainable success, businesses need to invest in reskilling their workforce, ensuring that employees can adapt to new, AI-driven processes while retaining the innovation that comes from human collaboration.

Impact on Other Stakeholders

1. Regulatory and Ethical Challenges

- As AI transforms industries and displaces jobs, governments and regulatory bodies will need to address the growing inequality and potential societal disruption. Policies to support displaced workers through retraining programs, and regulations governing the ethical use of AI, will become increasingly necessary.

2. Economic Inequality and Skills Gaps

- AI adoption is likely to widen the gap between high-skilled and low-skilled workers. High-skilled employees who can adapt to AI-driven roles will remain in demand, while those without the skills to interact with or manage AI systems may struggle to find employment. This will reinforce and worsen the digital gap, with high digital jobs already paying 140% more than low digital jobs ($73k vs. $30k)

- The challenge is ensuring that workers can reskill and retrain, so they remain competitive in an evolving job market. Governments, businesses, and educational institutions will need to work together to bridge this skills gap.

3. Broader Ecosystem Changes

- The adoption of AI also reshapes industries and ecosystems. Service-based industries, in particular, are seeing human-driven jobs like customer support or data entry increasingly replaced by AI-driven services. This shift leads to the reconfiguration of industry partnerships, as more companies rely on AI service providers to handle traditionally human tasks.

Conclusion

The primary impact of Cheaper, Better, Faster AI is clear: mass job displacement in roles that are routine, repetitive, and predictable. However, the secondary impacts are equally important: the augmentation of certain jobs and the creation of entirely new roles. After addressing the fundamental shift in the job market, we can see how this transformation also affects employers, other stakeholders, and the broader economy.

To fully navigate the impact of AI, both companies and employees must focus on reskilling and retraining, ensuring that they can adapt to a world where AI plays an ever-increasing role in the workforce.

1. UNBUNDLING

2. COMPETITION

3. WINNER-TAKES-ALL

4. REBUNDLING

The Enhancing Impact on jobs

In the Enhancing AI model, the focus shifts from competition to collaboration. Rather than displacing workers, Enhancing AI aims to augment human capabilities, empowering employees to perform more complex tasks with the assistance of AI. This model isn't about making tasks simply cheaper or faster; it's about enabling workers to do things they couldn't do before — like handling larger data sets, coding with minimal technical expertise, or delivering more insightful analysis.

For AI disruptors, this means the challenge is not to replace human labour but to find areas where AI can add value — increasing worker productivity, enhancing decision-making, and supporting more efficient workflows. The focus here is on specific, narrow tasks within jobs that benefit from automation, but still require human oversight. AI steps in to handle routine or data-intensive parts of a task, allowing workers to focus on higher-level thinking, strategy, or creativity. This symbiotic relationship between humans and AI highlights the potential of augmented roles where both AI and human expertise are necessary to achieve optimal outcomes.

The Enhancing AI Impact on Jobs: The Perspective of the AI Disruptor

In the Enhancing AI model, the focus shifts away from direct competition with human workers (as seen in the Cheaper, Better, Faster approach) and towards collaboration. For AI disruptors in this space, the goal is not to replace humans but to work alongside them, augmenting their abilities and making them more productive. It's about finding the right customers and processes where AI can assist workers in performing narrow, defined tasks that still require human oversight and decision-making.

Enhancing AI: Not About Competing, But Supporting

From the perspective of the AI provider, Enhancing AI is about identifying processes where AI can support employees rather than fully automate their roles. Unlike Cheaper/Better/Faster AI, where the goal is to replace human work with more efficient automation, Enhancing AI focuses on augmenting specific tasks within a job that benefit from AI's strengths — such as data processing, basic coding, or predictive analysis — while leaving the strategic or creative elements to human employees.

For AI disruptors, the strategy is to augment human capabilities in areas where AI excels at speed and efficiency but still needs human interpretation or final decision-making. This model allows for narrower tasks to be offloaded to AI, enabling human workers to focus on higher-level tasks without losing their core responsibilities.

Finding the Right Markets for Enhancing AI

In the Enhancing AI model, the goal is not to outperform or replace human workers but to augment their abilities in specific, high-impact areas. For AI providers, the challenge is to identify target markets where AI can handle narrow tasks that still require human oversight or input, allowing employees to focus on more strategic aspects of their roles. This section will explore the types of industries and job functions where Enhancing AI can provide the greatest value, and how disruptors can strategically choose their target markets to make AI augmentation worthwhile.

Targeting Industries with High Human Oversight

Enhancing AI is most effective in industries where human judgement and creativity are still crucial but can be supported by AI's ability to handle data-driven, routine tasks. In these sectors, AI doesn't replace human workers but takes over specific parts of their workload, allowing them to deliver better results.

- **Consulting and Professional Services:** AI can assist consultants by performing data analysis, generating reports, or handling routine administrative work, allowing consultants to focus on delivering high-level strategic advice to clients. This is a clear example of AI augmenting rather than replacing roles.

- **Healthcare:** AI can assist doctors in analysing medical images or running diagnostic models, speeding up processes without replacing human medical judgement. In healthcare, Enhancing AI allows professionals to make more informed decisions while handling routine data-heavy tasks more efficiently.

Focus on Markets with a Large Addressable Scope

For Enhancing AI to make economic sense, the market must be large enough to justify the investment in AI tools. AI disruptors target industries or roles where there is a high demand for efficiency improvements, and AI can streamline specific parts of the job at scale.

- Customer Support: we've seen that customer service agents can be replaced by AI. However, there are also many other cases where customer service requires a human interaction, from complex products to a required level of service of trust. Here, AI can support agents with faster access to information or product suggestions.

- Financial Services: In sectors like banking or insurance, AI can help by analysing large data sets to make initial recommendations or flagging risks, but human professionals still make the final decisions, especially in high-stakes situations.

Tasks Requiring AI-Driven Augmentation

The sweet spot for Enhancing AI is in tasks that are too complex for full automation but can be improved through AI assistance. These are tasks that require AI's ability to handle data or perform routine functions at scale, while humans focus on making strategic decisions or providing creative input.

- Legal Research: AI can be used to scan large volumes of legal documents and precedents, providing lawyers with quicker access to relevant information, while the lawyers focus on interpretation and case strategy.

- Data-Heavy Roles: In industries like market research or auditing, AI can handle large-scale data collection and initial analysis, freeing up workers to focus on interpreting the results and delivering insights.

Focus on Augmentation, Not Replacement

In the Enhancing AI model, the disruptor doesn't need to outperform humans across the board. Instead, they need to target markets where AI can provide value by assisting workers in narrow, well-defined tasks. This could include areas like data entry, report generation, or automated analysis, where AI's speed and accuracy can augment human performance. The aim is to integrate AI into existing workflows, enabling workers to offload routine tasks to AI while focusing on highcr-order responsibilities such as decision-making and strategy.

For example, customer service agents using Generative AI tools can handle more calls per hour and resolve issues faster. However, human oversight remains critical for complex issues that require empathy or creative problem-solving.

The Importance of a Large Addressable Market

While Enhancing AI focuses on narrow tasks, the addressable market still needs to be large enough to make the investment worthwhile for AI providers. AI disruptors target sectors with high volumes of repeatable tasks that can be augmented, allowing the technology to scale efficiently across a wide range of applications. For instance:

- Customer support roles handle thousands of interactions daily, making them prime targets for AI augmentation.

- Consulting firms can use AI to assist in routine analysis or data processing, allowing consultants to manage larger projects with the same workforce.

By targeting these large, task-heavy markets, Enhancing AI disruptors can create value by boosting worker productivity without eliminating the need for human labour.

What Does Enhancing AI Look Like in Practice?

Enhancing AI focuses on boosting human productivity without replacing workers, making tasks easier or more efficient by augmenting human capabilities. The goal is to provide tools that help workers accomplish more while keeping human oversight and decision-making intact. Here are real-world examples of how Generative AI is transforming industries by enhancing workers' abilities:

BCG: Enhancing Consultant Capabilities with Generative AI

Boston Consulting Group (BCG) used Generative AI to enhance their consultants' capabilities by allowing them to perform tasks such as coding and data analysis, which are typically outside their areas of expertise. In a study involving 480 BCG consultants, the AI tools helped employees reach 86% of the performance benchmark of professional data scientists, compared to just 29% without AI assistance. Even consultants with no prior experience in technical tasks could achieve 84% of expert-level results using Generative AI tools. This significant productivity boost allowed consultants to handle complex data-driven projects more efficiently without needing to hire additional specialists.

However, the study also highlighted two limitations: first, consultants sometimes over-relied on AI, leading to mistakes when the AI misunderstood the task. This illustrates the importance of human oversight in ensuring accuracy and maintaining quality. Secondly, consultants who did well on these new tasks, went back to their initial base line as soon as they lost access to the tool. In other words, using AI didn't help them acquire new skills. This is why the authors call AI an **exoskeleton**, i.e. a machine that helps you carry weight, but doesn't make you personally stronger.

GitHub Copilot: Supercharging Developer Productivity

GitHub Copilot is another example of Enhancing AI in action. This tool assists developers by providing real-time code suggestions, enabling them to write code more efficiently. According to studies, developers using GitHub Copilot reported a 27% increase in productivity, particularly in repetitive tasks like writing routine code. By automating these basic tasks, developers could focus on more creative problem-solving and system design.

However, Copilot has its limitations: developers still need to carefully review and refine the AI-generated code to ensure correctness, especially when the suggestions are not entirely accurate. This highlights the need for developer oversight to ensure the code meets the desired quality and functionality

Generative AI in Customer Support: Boosting Efficiency Without Replacing Agents

A study by the National Bureau of Economic Research (NBER) examined how Generative AI impacted customer support agents at a Fortune 500 company. The introduction of AI tools resulted in a 14% increase in productivity across all agents, with novice workers seeing the biggest gains — improving their performance by 34%. The AI helped newer employees learn faster by mimicking the communication patterns of more experienced workers, enabling them to handle customer queries more effectively.

Interestingly, the AI not only improved productivity but also increased job satisfaction and employee retention, particularly among newer agents. Customers also responded more positively to AI-augmented agents, leading to better overall service quality. However, the study found minimal impact on highly experienced agents, suggesting that AI is most beneficial in enhancing the skills of less-experienced workers

The Appeal of Enhancing AI

In these examples, Enhancing AI doesn't replace workers — it empowers them to handle more complex tasks with greater efficiency. Consultants at BCG could deliver deeper insights, developers using GitHub Copilot could write code faster, and customer service agents became more effective at handling inquiries. The result is higher productivity, better job satisfaction, and improved service quality, all while keeping human oversight crucial for ensuring accuracy and quality control.

What This Means for Jobs

The primary impact of Enhancing AI is job augmentation. Workers are able to manage more challenging tasks with AI support, and they are also required to upskill to collaborate effectively with AI systems. The secondary impact is the emergence of new hybrid roles where employees both oversee and interact with AI tools to deliver enhanced outcomes. As AI continues to evolve, workers will be better equipped to take on more strategic roles, driving both productivity and innovation across industries.

Dynamics of Enhancing: Supercharged Professionals

Enhancing AI focuses on augmenting human capabilities rather than replacing workers outright, creating a different dynamic compared to Cheaper, Better, Faster AI. AI in this context improves efficiency, decision-making, and productivity, allowing employees to handle more complex tasks while offloading repetitive or low-skill tasks to AI systems. The adoption of Enhancing AI is driven by organisations seeking to optimise their workforce, rather than replace it.

AI will target sectors where augmentation is key, particularly in knowledge-intensive industries

Enhancing AI will first take hold in industries where employees are required to perform complex, high-value tasks, but need AI tools to support decision-making, manage large datasets, or improve workflow efficiency. Consulting, financial services, legal advisory, and pharmaceutical research are key sectors where AI's role is to act as a multiplier, boosting employee productivity rather than displacing them. For example, consultants using AI for data analysis can deliver deeper insights in less time, and researchers in pharmaceutical companies can use AI to run simulations and analyse complex datasets more efficiently.

Verticals most likely to benefit from Enhancing AI include:

- Healthcare: Doctors and researchers can use AI to augment diagnosis accuracy or conduct faster drug development without replacing human judgement.
- Consulting: Consultants can handle bigger datasets and more complex analysis in less time, improving client outcomes and expanding their ability to handle multiple projects at once.
- Financial Services: AI can analyse large financial datasets, help in risk assessment, and improve portfolio management by providing real-time insights that employees can act upon.

It starts with unbundling repetitive tasks, then expands to more complex, high-value roles

In the initial phase, Enhancing AI will target repetitive, data-driven tasks within knowledge-intensive jobs, allowing employees to automate lower-skill elements of their work. By freeing up time, workers can focus on higher-order tasks such as strategic decision-making and innovation. For example, in consulting, AI may first be used to handle data extraction and basic analysis, then gradually expand to areas like forecasting, market research, and client-specific insights.

Once AI systems prove reliable in augmenting these tasks, organisations will shift to rebundling — expanding AI use to more critical and complex functions. AI might be integrated into decision-making processes, helping employees make faster, more informed decisions based on vast data inputs. In pharmaceutical research, AI could initially handle data analysis before expanding to experiment planning and predictive modelling, enhancing the entire research process without replacing scientists.

Employers will cautiously welcome Enhancing AI as a productivity multiplier

Unlike Cheaper AI, which focuses on cost-cutting, Enhancing AI will be adopted by employers as a tool to improve employee productivity. The appeal for businesses lies in AI's ability to help employees achieve more without increasing headcount, thus maximising the efficiency of the current workforce.

For example, AI tools for consultants allow them to handle more data and provide deeper insights to clients, making consultants more valuable and improving overall client satisfaction. In research sectors like biotechnology, AI augments the capabilities of scientists and researchers, allowing them to analyse data and run simulations faster, which accelerates the pace of discovery while maintaining the importance of human judgement.

However, similarly to all technology implementations, employers will exercise caution to ensure that processes, governance or capabilities are being properly considered through change management.

Companies adopting Enhancing AI will see it as a way to:

- Increase output per employee: Employees can complete more complex tasks in less time with the help of AI tools.
- Reduce errors: AI's accuracy in data analysis reduces the chances of human error, leading to improved decision-making.
- Accelerate decision-making: AI enables faster analysis and insights, allowing for quicker strategic decisions.

Employees will also adopt AI, sometimes with initial reservation

Employees, particularly in knowledge-intensive industries, may initially approach Enhancing AI with caution, worried about their long-term relevance in a tech-driven environment. However, as the AI tools are being pushed by their employers, and most of them are easy to learn, the employees are most likely to adapt AI rapidly.

In many cases, employees who embrace AI will see their roles evolve into higher-order decision-making and strategic functions, while AI takes care of data processing or other time-consuming tasks. However, adaptation will require reskilling. Training programs and upskilling initiatives will be necessary to ensure that employees can effectively manage AI tools, interpret their outputs, and combine AI-driven insights with human judgement.

Regulatory and Stakeholder Reactions

Regulators will likely focus less on job displacement and more on ensuring the ethical use of AI, particularly around data privacy, bias in AI models, and the transparency of AI-assisted decision-making. For industries like healthcare or financial services, regulators will need to set standards for AI oversight, ensuring that human judgement remains an essential part of the process. Stakeholders, including employees and investors, may also question how AI enhances productivity without leading to over-reliance on technology, creating ethical and operational debates about where the human-AI balance should lie.

Impact (End Result) of Enhancing AI

The adoption of **Enhancing** AI fundamentally transforms not just individual roles but entire business operations. By augmenting human capabilities, AI allows employees to achieve more complex tasks with greater efficiency, creating both primary and secondary impacts. While AI boosts productivity, leading to job augmentation and new job opportunities, it can also reduce the need for certain roles, as fewer people may be required to manage the increased workload. Below is a breakdown of the impacts on jobs, employers, and the broader ecosystem.

Impact on Jobs (Primary and Secondary)

1. Primary Impact: Supercharged Professionals

- The most immediate effect of Enhancing AI is the augmentation of existing roles. Employees are not replaced by AI but rather empowered to work more efficiently. AI tools help automate repetitive tasks, allowing workers to focus on higher-order tasks such as strategy, decision-making, and creativity. These supercharged professionals are able to handle larger workloads and solve more complex problems thanks to AI's ability to take care of mundane or technical aspects of their jobs.

- Real-world example: at CFTE, our team has become supercharged since ChatGPT was launched. All employees are very proficient in many different AI tools – from generic LLMs to more specialised tools for content creation, video edition, even deepfakes or avatars. This has for example helped significantly decrease the time to create courses and the breadth of the product suite.

2. Secondary Impact: New Jobs and Job Losses

- New job creation is a significant secondary impact of Enhancing AI. As AI systems become central to business operations, entirely new roles such as AI specialists, data managers, and AI ethicists are created to oversee the integration of AI into workflows.

- Job loss is also a potential secondary impact, as AI enables companies to become much more productive with fewer workers. While AI augments existing roles, it can also lead to job cuts, especially in sectors where productivity improvements mean fewer people are required to achieve the same level of output. The common phrase **"you won't be replaced by AI, but by someone who uses AI"** highlights this dynamic, where AI-savvy employees may replace those unable to adapt.

- Real-world example: In customer service, Generative AI tools help human agents handle more inquiries per hour, potentially reducing the need for large customer support teams. Fewer workers may be needed as productivity rises, even though the remaining staff are delivering enhanced, AI-assisted service.

2. Shift in Skill Requirements

- As jobs evolve, employees will need to adapt to these changes by developing new skills. The workforce will shift toward roles that require AI management, problem-solving, creativity, and emotional intelligence — tasks that AI cannot easily replicate. Workers must engage in continuous upskilling to remain competitive in an AI-enhanced environment, with an emphasis on mastering how to collaborate with AI systems.

- Companies that invest in reskilling will have a more versatile workforce, capable of leveraging AI to optimise business processes while keeping the human touch where it's needed.

Impact on Employers (Customers)

1. Increased Productivity

- Employers see immediate productivity gains as AI handles repetitive tasks and employees are freed to focus on more complex work. This boosts overall efficiency without the need to increase headcount, making AI a highly attractive investment for businesses.

- Example: In financial services, AI helps professionals manage larger datasets and make quicker decisions, allowing firms to handle more clients with the same number of employees.

2. Revenue Per Employee

- AI-enhanced employees contribute to a rise in revenue per employee. By automating routine tasks, employees can complete more valuable work in less time, driving overall profitability.

- Example: AI tools in marketing can automate customer segmentation and personalised content creation, allowing teams to launch more campaigns with fewer staff members, ultimately increasing company revenue.

3. Innovation and Competitive Advantage

- Over the medium and long term, companies that adopt Enhancing AI gain a competitive edge. By allowing employees to focus on high-value tasks such as innovation and strategy, businesses can differentiate themselves in the marketplace with more creative solutions and advanced services.

- Example: In the healthcare sector, AI helps doctors focus on patient care while the AI manages diagnostics and data analysis, giving hospitals a competitive edge in providing faster and more accurate services.

Impact on Products (Jobs) and Services

1. Higher Quality Outputs

- AI improves the quality of work by reducing errors and handling data-intensive tasks, allowing employees to focus on strategy and creativity. This enhances product development and service delivery across industries, leading to better outcomes for both businesses and customers.

- Example: In legal services, AI can handle document review and research, enabling lawyers to spend more time on case strategy and client relations, leading to improved service quality.

2. Scalability with Human Oversight

- Enhancing AI allows businesses to scale operations without proportionally increasing their workforce. While AI handles the repetitive tasks, human oversight ensures that the final outputs maintain high quality. This model allows companies to grow while maintaining human oversight for complex decision-making and customer interaction.

- Example: Pharmaceutical companies can use AI to scale research efforts, with scientists overseeing the AI's output

203

to ensure accuracy and compliance with regulatory standards.

Impact on Other Stakeholders

1. Ethical and Regulatory Considerations
- As AI becomes embedded in workflows, regulatory bodies will need to ensure the ethical use of AI, addressing issues such as bias, data privacy, and AI accountability. Maintaining human oversight will be crucial in industries where transparency and fairness are essential.

2. Workforce Transformation
- AI will lead to significant workforce transformation, with hybrid roles becoming the norm. Employees will need to become AI-literate to succeed in these roles, and companies will need to invest in retraining programs to bridge the skills gap and ensure their workforce remains competitive.

Conclusion

The impact of Enhancing AI goes beyond job augmentation — it reshapes industries, workforce dynamics, and operational scalability. By supercharging professionals, creating new jobs, and reducing the need for some roles, AI is driving a significant transformation in how businesses and employees operate. The need for upskilling, continuous learning, and a strong focus on ethical oversight will be critical for both businesses and employees to thrive in an AI-augmented future.

I. UNBUNDLING

II. ENTERPRISE SALES

III. LONG SALES CYCLE

IV. REBUNDLING

The Different (D) Impact on Jobs

Introduction: Shaping New Possibilities with Different

When it comes to Different (D), predicting its impact is notoriously difficult — but this is precisely what makes it so exciting. Different AI, much like other disruptive innovations in history, has the potential to completely transform industries and even create entirely new ecosystems. Consider the early days of Facebook, Google, or the launch of the iPhone. At the time, it would have been impossible to fully grasp the scale of their impact, not just as companies, but in how they created entire ecosystems around them. They transformed our behaviours, changed how we interact with the world, and even reshaped our ways of thinking.

For example, few could have predicted how Facebook would revolutionise social interaction or how Google would redefine the way we access information. Similarly, Bitcoin disrupted traditional financial systems by introducing the concept of decentralised currency, and the iPhone did more than just give us a smartphone — it reshaped entire industries, from apps to mobile commerce. These innovations didn't just create new products; they changed the rules of the game, sparking revolutions across industries.

We are currently standing at a similar moment with AI. We know that Different AI will lead to disruptions and transformations, but it's difficult to foresee exactly what these innovations will be or how far their impact will reach. Just as it was hard to imagine the long-term consequences of the Internet in the 1990s, we can't yet fully anticipate the ways in which AI will reshape industries and society.

However, one thing is clear: many of these Different innovations will begin with new products — products that challenge what we know and introduce entirely new ways of solving problems. The disruptors in this space will be those

206

who create products that are totally novel — innovations that we may not yet fully understand, but which will undoubtedly shape the future.

We've already seen glimpses of this with breakthroughs like AlphaFold 2, which revolutionised protein folding (earning a Nobel Prize) and is set to change the future of drug discovery. Other groundbreaking technologies, such as self-driving cars and Brain-Computer Interfaces (BCI), are beginning to show the world what's possible when AI is applied to areas once thought out of reach for machines. Some even believe that the most transformative innovation will be the advent of Artificial General Intelligence (AGI), a form of AI that may one day rival human intelligence itself.

In short, Different AI is where we'll see the biggest leaps in innovation — ones that will not only disrupt individual industries but may fundamentally alter how we live and think. While the full extent of its impact is unpredictable, what we do know is that it will challenge our understanding of what is possible.

Defining Different AI: The Perspective of the AI Disruptor

Different AI refers to innovations that fundamentally change the way we think, work, and live by introducing new products, services, and business models that didn't exist before. Unlike innovations that focus on improving efficiency or enhancing current operations, Different AI disrupts the status quo by offering something entirely novel — from products that revolutionise industries to services that redefine entire ecosystems.

The disruptors who create these innovations are not just competing in existing markets — they're creating new markets altogether. Whether it's launching self-driving cars, developing personalised AI-generated content, or crafting breakthrough biomedical solutions, Different AI transforms industries in ways that weren't previously possible. Just like the early days of Facebook, Bitcoin, or the iPhone, the full scale of their future impact can be hard to predict at the outset.

Examples of Different AI innovations include:

- AlphaFold 2, which revolutionised protein folding and earned a Nobel Prize for its groundbreaking impact on drug discovery.

- Self-driving cars, which are creating new possibilities for autonomous transportation.

- Brain-Computer Interfaces (BCI), which allow for direct communication between the human brain and machines, opening up unprecedented opportunities in healthcare and beyond.

- And of course, the Different innovation that has had the most impact on all of us so far: Large Language Models and Generative AI such as ChatGPT.

The role of the AI disruptor here is to anticipate unmet needs and create something entirely new, not just improve what's already there. These innovations don't just solve current problems; they change the way we think about those problems entirely.

Different Types of Innovation: What Sets Different AI Apart?

Different AI is not about incremental improvements or making existing processes faster, cheaper, or more efficient. It's about creating new opportunities that were unimaginable before AI's arrival. These innovations go beyond conventional boundaries and open up new paradigms for industries, often requiring entirely new ways of thinking.

Many disruptive innovations throughout history followed this path. Google started as a search engine but evolved into a tech giant that redefined how we think about information, data, and connectivity. Facebook reshaped the way we interact with each other globally, and the iPhone redefined mobile computing, spawning entire ecosystems like the App Store.

In the same way, Different AI has the potential to:

- Create new product categories: AI can generate new forms of media (such as AI-generated films, music, and art) that challenge traditional definitions of creativity.

- Disrupt traditional industries: AI may lead to the emergence of personalised medicine based on genetic data, which could transform healthcare into a precision science.

- Redefine interaction with technology: AI-driven tools like Brain-Computer Interfaces could change how we interact with machines, making futuristic concepts like controlling devices with our thoughts a reality.

These innovations are hard to predict, but their disruptive potential is immense. They're not about optimising or enhancing the existing — they're about doing something entirely new.

The Product-Market Fit of Different AI

For AI disruptors working in this space, achieving product-market fit means identifying where AI can create something truly novel — where it opens up entirely new business models, products, or experiences that don't yet exist.

Key criteria for Different AI product-market fit include:

1. **Radically new capabilities**: The innovation must do something that was previously impossible or that fundamentally alters how we approach a problem. Whether it's AI models creating lifelike art, predicting diseases, or allowing machines to interpret human thoughts, the technology must provide capabilities that offer a clear leap forward.

2. **Untapped markets**: Different AI thrives where new business opportunities arise. These often involve emerging sectors or applications where AI is the critical enabler. For instance, autonomous transportation (self-driving cars) or AI in drug discovery are examples of new markets created by AI's unique capabilities.

Examples of successful product-market fit include:

- AI in Healthcare: AI-driven platforms that develop personalised treatments based on a patient's genetic information, such as AlphaFold 2, are transforming medicine by making precision healthcare a reality.

- AI-Generated Media: Platforms like DALL☐E and GPT-4 have given rise to AI-generated art, stories, and even video games, creating entirely new markets for AI-driven creativity.

- Autonomous Vehicles: Companies like Waymo have developed AI systems that drive cars autonomously, creating a new industry around self-driving technology and changing the future of transportation.

For AI disruptors, product-market fit isn't just about improving existing solutions. It's about identifying where AI opens new doors and creates opportunities that previously seemed out of reach.

What Does Different AI Look Like in Practice?

Different AI goes beyond optimising existing tasks or enhancing human abilities — it creates entirely new possibilities. From transforming drug discovery to revolutionising transportation and human-computer interaction, Different AI is about exploring uncharted territory. But with these innovations comes a reshaping of the job market — creating new roles, transforming existing ones, and displacing others. Let's dive into three real-world examples of how Different AI is reshaping industries and the jobs within them.

210

1. AlphaFold 2: Revolutionising Drug Discovery

One of the most groundbreaking examples of Different AI is AlphaFold 2. Developed by DeepMind, AlphaFold 2 solved the protein-folding problem — a major scientific breakthrough that has immense implications for drug discovery and biotechnology. By accurately predicting the structure of proteins, which are fundamental to biological processes, AlphaFold 2 has drastically reduced the time and cost associated with experimental research.

Impact on Jobs

AlphaFold 2 has introduced entirely new job roles, such as AI-driven biotech specialists who combine deep expertise in biology with machine learning skills to integrate AI into drug discovery pipelines. Bioinformatics analysts are also in high demand to interpret the vast amounts of data that AI like AlphaFold generates. These roles didn't exist in the same capacity before AI came into the picture, creating a hybrid field where biology and AI intersect.

While it has created new opportunities, AlphaFold 2 has also displaced more traditional lab-based roles. Tasks that once took years of experimental research can now be done in days using AI. This shift is leading to a reduction in the need for manual protein-folding technicians and experimental biologists who traditionally handled these processes in the lab. However, rather than eliminating jobs altogether, these roles are evolving — many researchers are now working alongside AI to leverage its speed and accuracy.

Transformation of Roles

For biologists and drug developers, AlphaFold 2 has transformed the nature of their work. Instead of spending extensive time in labs running experiments, they now focus more on interpreting AI-generated results and applying these insights to develop new drugs and treatments. This requires professionals to gain new skills in data science and AI literacy, blending traditional biological expertise with advanced computational tools.

2. Autonomous Vehicles: The Self-Driving Revolution

Autonomous vehicles (AVs) are fundamentally altering the transportation industry. Companies like Waymo and Tesla are leading the way with AI-powered self-driving cars that can navigate roads with minimal human intervention. The potential impact of AVs goes far beyond personal transport, affecting logistics, ride-sharing, and even city planning.

Impact on Jobs

What would happen to jobs if cars, taxis and trucks were driverless? Truck drivers, taxi drivers, and delivery personnel would definitely the most affected, as AI performs their roles with greater efficiency and fewer errors. The rise of autonomous delivery fleets is already reducing the demand for human drivers in some sectors, and this trend is expected to accelerate as AV technology improves.

However, AVs are also creating new opportunities. Jobs like fleet managers for autonomous vehicles are emerging to monitor, maintain, and optimise AV operations. These managers work with AI systems to ensure vehicles are running smoothly, requiring a new skill set that blends logistics with AI system management. In addition, AI safety specialists are becoming increasingly important, tasked with ensuring that AVs meet safety and ethical standards, particularly in emergency decision-making scenarios.

Transformation of Roles

The introduction of AVs is transforming roles in urban planning and logistics management. Urban planners are rethinking city layouts to accommodate self-driving vehicles, including designing smart roads and AV-only lanes. Logistics managers are adapting by integrating autonomous vehicles into supply chains, focusing less on managing drivers and more on coordinating AI-powered delivery fleets.

While many traditional driving jobs are at risk, there is also potential for new opportunities in maintaining and programming autonomous fleets. The workforce will need to transition from manual driving roles to overseeing and managing the technology that powers autonomous transport.

3. Brain-Computer Interfaces (BCI): The New Frontier of Human-AI Interaction

Brain-Computer Interfaces (BCIs), pioneered by companies like Neuralink and Kernel, represent a cutting-edge intersection of neuroscience and AI. BCIs allow direct communication between the brain and external devices, enabling control of computers, robotic limbs, and other systems through thought alone. This technology has the potential to revolutionise healthcare, gaming, and even how we interact with machines in everyday life.

Impact on Jobs

The emergence of BCIs has created new roles in fields such as neurotechnology and AI-assisted rehabilitation. Neurotechnologists are responsible for designing and developing the hardware and software that make BCIs possible. These professionals work at the intersection of neuroscience, AI, and biomedical engineering. Additionally, AI-integrated therapists now assist patients in using BCIs for rehabilitation, helping them recover motor functions or communicate through AI-enabled devices.

However, the rise of BCIs could also reduce demand for more traditional assistive technology roles. For instance, jobs related to the maintenance of manual assistive devices, such as wheelchairs and hearing aids, may decline as BCIs become more widespread and effective. Traditional physical therapists may see their roles evolve as BCIs enable more advanced forms of neurorehabilitation that go beyond manual therapy.

Transformation of Roles

In the gaming and entertainment industries, BCIs are set to transform the roles of game designers and interactive experience developers. Instead of designing games controlled by physical devices, developers will need to think about how players interact using their brain activity, opening up new avenues for immersive gaming experiences. Similarly, rehabilitation specialists are transitioning from purely manual techniques to using AI-powered devices that respond to brain signals, providing a more tailored and efficient recovery process for patients.

Conclusion: The Transformative Power of Different AI on Jobs

The examples of AlphaFold 2, autonomous vehicles, and BCIs show how Different AI is not just about creating new technologies, but about reshaping the job market in fundamental ways. While it creates exciting new opportunities, it also transforms and displaces existing roles. The introduction of AI into these sectors means that workers must adapt, reskill, and evolve to stay relevant in a world where AI is a core driver of innovation.

Different AI is pushing industries toward a future where collaboration between humans and machines is essential. This collaboration, however, will lead to both job creation in emerging fields and job displacement in traditional sectors. For professionals across industries, the key to thriving in this new AI-driven landscape will be the ability to continuously learn, adapt, and collaborate with these advanced systems.

The Dynamics of Different AI: A Future Shaped by Creative Disruptors

Different AI is fundamentally about creating possibilities that don't yet exist, which makes predicting its future impact both challenging and fascinating. Unlike more straightforward AI innovations — such as automation and augmentation, where we can reasonably foresee shifts in job roles and efficiency gains — Different AI is about foresight and future thinking. It pushes the boundaries of human creativity, leading to disruptions that can't be easily predicted, but which will likely come from a small number of creative polymaths capable of cross-discipline thinking.

The Rise of Creative Disruptors

In a world driven by Different innovations, the individuals who will have the most impact will be those who can think and innovate across multiple domains, merging insights from various fields into something entirely new. This is a departure from the past, where the most influential figures were often specialists in a single discipline. As the world becomes more interconnected and AI tools make it easier to access information across different areas of expertise, the future belongs to polymaths — those with a broad range of skills spanning multiple disciplines.

Take Demis Hassabis, for example. The founder of DeepMind, he is both a neuroscientist and computer scientist, and his deep understanding of how the human brain works informed his groundbreaking work in AI. Another example is Elon Musk, whose impact spans industries as diverse as space exploration (SpaceX), electric vehicles (Tesla), and brain-computer interfaces (Neuralink). These polymaths are capable of weaving together insights from different fields, enabling them to create innovations that disrupt entire industries, not just individual sectors.

In the future, more polymath-like individuals — with deep knowledge of fields like AI, biology, neuroscience, engineering, perhaps even philosophy! — are likely to emerge as the drivers of change. These creative disruptors will use AI not just as a tool to optimise processes but as a partner in invention, leading to the development of products, services, and even industries that we can't yet imagine.

Different AI and Cross-Disciplinary Innovation

Different AI thrives on cross-disciplinary thinking. The most transformative innovations are likely to come from those who can blend insights from disparate fields, making connections between areas of expertise that traditionally operated in isolation. In this sense, the future of AI-driven innovation won't just be about creating more efficient tools but about redefining industries through unexpected combinations of knowledge.

For example:

- AlphaFold 2 emerged from the intersection of biology and AI, solving a problem that had stumped biologists for decades. The future could see more of these interdisciplinary breakthroughs, where the combination of biology, computing, and data science leads to the development of entirely new forms of medicine, personalised healthcare, and genomic treatments.

- Brain-Computer Interfaces (BCIs), being developed by companies like Neuralink, rely on insights from neuroscience, engineering, and AI. The people driving these innovations aren't specialists in one area — they're navigating between fields, applying AI to human-machine interfaces in ways that could transform healthcare, gaming, and communication.

This ability to bring together disparate fields will be critical to the success of Different AI disruptors. These individuals and teams will need to harness the full spectrum of human knowledge to create AI systems that can redefine industries and reshape human interaction with technology.

The Role of AI-Enhanced Creativity

In this new landscape, AI will not just enhance human creativity; it will actively partner with creative minds to invent entirely new products and services. These polymath-like innovators will increasingly leverage AI to explore ideas, simulate outcomes, and accelerate the innovation process.

One significant shift we're likely to see is that AI-enhanced creativity will enable individuals to invent, prototype, and deploy new concepts much faster than ever before. The ability to work with AI tools that can perform rapid simulations, generate new designs, or suggest creative solutions will allow these disruptors to experiment and iterate with unprecedented speed.

Example:

- In architecture, future creative disruptors may use AI not just to design buildings but to simulate how different materials, forms, and designs will interact with the environment, leading to entirely new approaches to urban design and sustainable cities.

- In biotechnology, AI could help creative disruptors rapidly test new drug formulations in silico (using simulations), predicting the effects before any physical trials are conducted.

217

The Ecosystem Effect: From Innovators to Industry Transformations

The impact of creative polymaths will extend beyond their own inventions. Just as Facebook didn't just create a social network but an entire ecosystem of businesses that revolve around social media, Different AI disruptors will lay the groundwork for entire new industries. These innovations will catalyse the development of new markets, jobs, and ecosystems, each requiring different skills and expertise.

- Autonomous Vehicles (AVs): AV technology, while driven by AI, is giving rise to entirely new industries, such as AI-driven logistics, smart city infrastructure, and autonomous fleet management. While traditional driving jobs may decline, new opportunities in AI fleet management, maintenance, and AI safety will emerge.

- BCIs and Neurotechnology: Brain-Computer Interfaces could lead to industries focused on neuro-assistive technologies, creating roles in neuroscience-driven tech and human-AI interaction specialists. These fields didn't exist a decade ago but may become some of the most sought-after professions in the coming years.

In this future, AI disruptors will create the tools, but it will be the surrounding ecosystem — companies, startups, and industries — that scale these innovations, transforming sectors and creating new job markets.

Foresight and Adaptability: Preparing for the Unknown

Because Different AI operates at the frontier of human creativity and technological progress, the future remains highly unpredictable. However, foresight and adaptability will be key. Both businesses and individuals will need to be agile in order to succeed in a world where the pace of AI-driven innovation continues to accelerate.

For organisations, this means investing in cross-disciplinary teams that are prepared to navigate complex, interconnected problems. For individuals, it means cultivating a polymathic mindset — not just being good at one thing, but being able to blend knowledge from various fields to see opportunities others may miss.

Conclusion: A Future Shaped by Creative Disruptors

As Different AI continues to push boundaries, the dynamics of the future will be shaped by creative polymaths — individuals who can operate across disciplines, blending insights from neuroscience, AI, biology, and beyond. These disruptors will not only transform industries but create entirely new ones, shifting the focus from specialisation to cross-disciplinary innovation.

The most influential figures in this space will be those who can think broadly and deeply, harnessing AI as a creative partner to invent new products, services, and systems that redefine our world. While the exact trajectory of Different AI is unpredictable, the individuals who will lead this charge are those who embrace the challenge of innovation at the intersection of multiple fields — those who can invent faster, integrate AI into their creative processes, and have an outsized impact on the future of industries and society as a whole.

Impact of Different AI: Ecosystems, Jobs, and Industry Transformation

Different AI innovations have the potential to do more than just improve processes or enhance productivity — they can create entirely new ecosystems. These ecosystems include new markets, industries, and whole networks of jobs that didn't exist before. Unlike AI models focused on cost-cutting or enhancing human roles, Different AI introduces novel technologies that require the creation of new professions, transformations in existing roles, and the eventual displacement of some traditional jobs. The most significant impact of Different AI will be felt in the way it redefines how industries function and how jobs evolve in response to these changes.

Impact on Jobs (Creation of New Ecosystems)

1. **New Job Creation**
- Different AI drives the creation of jobs in industries that don't yet exist. Just as the Internet created entire sectors like e-commerce, social media management, and app development, Different AI innovations will foster new professional fields. These jobs will likely focus on AI design, implementation, and oversight but also expand into niche areas tied to the specific disruptions introduced by AI.

- Example: In the healthcare sector, AI innovations like AlphaFold 2 and personalised medicine will lead to the rise of new roles such as genomic analysts, AI-driven biotech researchers, and AI treatment designers. These professionals will be at the forefront of combining biology, genetics, and AI to create new forms of medicine and treatment plans.

2. **Cross-Disciplinary Roles**
- Different AI demands new job types that sit at the intersection of multiple disciplines. For instance, a person working in brain-computer interfaces (BCIs) will need to understand both neuroscience and AI development, creating hybrid roles that span traditional domains. This polymathic demand will extend across sectors, as professionals capable of working across biology, AI, engineering, and design will be required to develop and manage the new AI-driven technologies.

- Example: In the case of BCIs, there will be demand for neurotechnology experts who combine insights from brain science and AI to develop cutting-edge applications, whether for healthcare, gaming, or human augmentation. These professionals will need to be proficient in understanding neural signals while also coding AI algorithms that can process brain activity.

2. Transformation of Existing Jobs

- Different AI doesn't just create new jobs; it also transforms existing ones. Roles that previously relied on manual or repetitive tasks will shift toward more creative, strategic, or oversight functions, as AI takes over routine elements of the job.

- Example: In drug discovery, the role of the biologist has transformed. Traditional lab work is increasingly supplemented by AI tools like AlphaFold 2, allowing biologists to focus on interpreting AI-generated data and making higher-level decisions about drug development. Similarly, in urban planning, the rise of autonomous vehicles will force planners to rethink city infrastructure, transforming their roles from traditional planning to smart city development that integrates AI-powered transport systems.

2. Job Displacement

- With the rise of Different AI, some traditional jobs will be displaced as entire sectors become automated or reinvented. This displacement will occur mainly in roles that AI can fully automate or make obsolete through its ability to perform tasks more efficiently or innovatively than humans.

- Example: In the transportation industry, the advent of autonomous vehicles could displace millions of professional drivers as self-driving trucks, taxis, and delivery vehicles reduce the need for human-operated transport. Similarly, routine jobs in experimental biology could be diminished as AI takes over protein folding, drug testing, and other experimental tasks that previously required human intervention.

Impact on Employers (New Industry Leadership and Innovation)

1. Industry Leadership and Competitive Edge

- Companies that successfully integrate Different AI into their business models will be poised to become industry leaders. By creating new products and services that set them apart, these companies will dominate their sectors, redefining what it means to compete.

- Example: The rise of Waymo and other companies developing autonomous vehicles shows how AI can give businesses a competitive edge. These companies aren't just making better cars — they're transforming transportation itself, leading in both innovation and market control.

2. Creation of Entirely New Markets

- Different AI doesn't just improve existing markets — it creates new ones. Employers can develop business models based on AI-native products or services that didn't exist before AI, ranging from AI-generated content platforms to AI-driven medical technologies. The first movers in these markets will have significant control over how these new industries evolve.

- Example: Companies like DeepMind are leading the way in AI-driven scientific research, which opens up new markets in personalised drug discovery and AI-assisted biotech. Similarly, AI-generated art and media platforms are starting to create new content-driven ecosystems where human creativity and AI merge to produce products at a scale and speed unimaginable before.

Impact on Products (Creating New Types of Products and Services)

1. New Product Categories

- Different AI allows companies to create entirely new product categories that weren't previously possible. From AI-generated music and art to autonomous transport

222

systems, these innovations aren't just improvements — they redefine what a product can be.

- Example: AI-generated content platforms, such as those powered by models like GPT-4 or DALL E, allow for the rapid creation of text, images, and videos with minimal human input. These products are not simply faster versions of existing content but entirely new categories of AI-driven creativity.

2. Hyper-Personalization and Tailored Solutions

- AI innovations will make products and services highly personalised in ways that were previously impractical. Different AI allows for solutions tailored to an individual's exact needs — whether in healthcare, entertainment, or finance.

- Example: In healthcare, AI-driven personalised medicine uses individual genetic profiles to design specific treatment plans, moving away from one-size-fits-all approaches to create more effective and targeted healthcare solutions.

Impact on Other Stakeholders

1. Regulatory and Ethical Considerations

- The creation of new AI-driven ecosystems will also raise regulatory challenges. Governments and regulators will need to establish frameworks for the ethical use of AI, particularly as these innovations reshape industries.

- Example: In industries like autonomous driving and BCIs, there are questions around liability, privacy, and safety. Governments will need to develop new policies that address these concerns while ensuring innovation can continue.

2. Shifts in Consumer Expectations

- As new products and services emerge from Different AI, consumer expectations will shift. Consumers will demand greater personalization, faster service, and more innovative products, pushing companies to keep up with these changing preferences.

- Example: AI-driven platforms that offer highly personalised content recommendations, like Spotify or Netflix, have already shifted how consumers interact with media. As AI expands into new markets, similar shifts in expectations will happen across industries.

Conclusion: The Impact of AI on Jobs

In this chapter, we've highlighted how AI's impact on jobs has become incredibly personal. This has made questions about employment and the future of work some of the most important topics of our time. However, because the impact feels so personal, it's also easy to get caught up in confusion and uncertainty. We often struggle to make sense of AI's role in our careers, leading to widespread concerns about job security and future opportunities.

This is where changing our perspective becomes crucial. Rather than looking at AI's effects solely from a personal or job-specific standpoint, it's more useful to adopt a broader, systems-level view. By shifting our focus and applying the CDE Innovation Prism and the EDGE Canvas, we can better structure our thinking around AI's impact. These frameworks help us move beyond the emotional responses and provide a clearer picture of the dynamics at play.

Through this approach, we've identified three key trends that are likely to shape the future of work in the age of AI:

- **Mass displacement**: AI will automate many jobs, especially those with repetitive tasks, leading to a shift in the workforce as certain roles are replaced by technology.
- **Supercharged professionals**: Some jobs won't be replaced but enhanced by AI, enabling professionals to achieve more, increase productivity, and focus on higher-level tasks.

- **Creative disruptors**: AI will also open entirely new industries and job roles, creating opportunities for individuals to lead innovation and work in areas that don't yet exist.

These trends are profound and far-reaching, representing both opportunities and risks. The risks — such as job displacement — will need to be carefully managed, and we must think strategically about how to prepare the workforce for this transformation. On the other hand, there are significant opportunities to leverage AI for personal and societal benefit.

The real value of this approach is that it simplifies the complexity of AI's impact and allows us to better understand the dynamics between AI as the **disruptor**, the **customers** who adopt AI solutions, and us as **workers**. By understanding these relationships, we can move from fear and confusion toward a more proactive stance — one that lets us shape our future with AI.

The next section will analyse 3 specific cases studies of AI **competing** with customer service agents (Klarna), **collaborating** with consultants (BCG) and **creating** totally new sectors (Alphafold).

And in the next chapter, we will explore what it means to be in a world where the three trends of mass displacement, supercharged professionals and creative disruptors come together. And what we, as individuals, policymakers and industry leaders, can do to actively shape our future.

I. VISION

II. PRODUCT INNOVATION

III. FIND BUSINESS MODEL

IV. UNPREDICTIBLE OUTCOME

Case Studies

Klarna, BCG and AlphaFold

For Klarna, AI was cheaper, better, faster (than its employees...)

In August 2023, Klarna's CEO Sebastian Siemiatkowski announced that the company had become the first in Europe to adopt ChatGPT Enterprise. Klarna, known for its Buy Now, Pay Later (BNPL) services, was rapidly integrating AI across its operations, with more than 50% of its employees using it daily, particularly in customer service, marketing, and legal departments.

Klarna's use of AI as a disruptor resulted in a significant transformation, with clear goals of increasing efficiency, reducing costs, and scaling the business ahead of its anticipated IPO. One of the first changes occurred in customer service, where Klarna's AI assistant transformed the way it interacted with customers, delivering faster, better, and cheaper services.

In February 2024, it announced that it had rolled out Generative AI as a chatbot, replacing the work of 700 customer service agents, saving $40 million per year, and increasing customer satisfaction.

In other words, this is a typical case of AI being cheaper, faster and better than the incumbent, i.e. humans.

Let's review the Klarna use case with the EDGE canvas:

Edge Analysis of replacing customer service agents by AI

E   D   G   E

Existing Ecosystem: the Customer is the employer, the Incumbent is the employee

E   D   G   E

- Customers: In this case, Klarna itself is the customer, with its internal operations benefiting from AI integration. As Klarna handles 2 million transactions per day, customer service is a crucial component of its activities, and used to employ 20% of its workforce. Initially, Klarna focused on growth, market share, and sales. However, with the company preparing for its IPO and a shifting market focus towards profitability, it began prioritising cost efficiency and sought AI solutions to streamline operations, particularly in customer service.

- Product: The product in question is customer service. This involves handling interactions between Klarna and its customers through various channels such as its website, mobile app, and call centres. Because Klarna is present in more than 40 countries, customer service had to be available in different languages, across different time zones.

- Incumbents: The incumbents in this case are Klarna's customer service agents. These employees were responsible for managing customer inquiries, including tasks like refunds, returns, and payment disputes. In 2023, many of these jobs were already outsourced to companies like Foundever and Accenture to cut costs. AI further displaced these incumbents by outperforming human agents in terms of speed, cost, and efficiency.

- Other Stakeholders: Klarna's clients, who interact through customer service channels, also represent key stakeholders, as their experience was directly affected by the transition to AI. In addition, regulators such as the Swedish Financial Supervisory Authority and the UK Financial Conduct Authority are important stakeholders, particularly given the significant changes in the workforce and the ethical considerations around AI adoption.

Disruptor: AI is the new entrant

The disruptor in Klarna's transformation is Artificial Intelligence (AI), specifically the AI assistant developed in collaboration with OpenAI. This assistant was integrated into Klarna's systems, managing routine tasks that previously required human intervention. The AI assistant could handle customer queries, resolve disputes, and provide real-time updates, outperforming human agents by reducing resolution time from 11 minutes to 2 minutes. Additionally, the AI operates 24/7, across 23 markets, and communicates in 35 languages — something human agents could not achieve at the same scale and cost.

Dynamics: A three-tiered dynamics between AI push, employer pull and employee pushback

Disruptor Push:

As the disruptor, OpenAI entered the highly competitive customer service space — a traditional human-led field — with a clear strategy: to outperform and replace existing human roles by offering a product vastly superior in terms of speed, availability, and scalability. In that strategy, competition is fierce, and the goal is to differentiate by creating a product that provides significantly better value or greater efficiency than the incumbents. OpenAI aims to deliver a service that not only matches but exceeds human capabilities in customer service, addressing pain points such as limited hours of operation, the need for multilingual support, and inconsistent response times.

OpenAI initially followed an unbundling strategy, focusing on specific, high-frequency customer service tasks — such as managing refunds, resolving payment disputes, and answering routine inquiries — that were traditionally managed by human agents. By isolating these core functions, OpenAI was able to develop an AI solution highly specialised in these repetitive tasks. This targeted approach allowed OpenAI to demonstrate that AI could handle these essential customer interactions faster and more accurately, without the costs associated with hiring, training, and managing a large team of human agents.

Once the AI proved effective in customer service, it moved into the rebundling phase. Having established a foothold in routine customer service, OpenAI expanded its applications across other areas within Klarna, such as marketing.

From a business perspective, OpenAI's success with Klarna positions it as a model for future AI-driven customer service transformations. Klarna's experience acts as a successful case study that OpenAI can leverage to market its solution globally. The ability to handle complex tasks at scale while reducing costs makes this AI highly attractive to companies with large customer service operations, suggesting that OpenAI is likely to push this solution to other clients worldwide.

Customer Pull:

As the Customer, Klarna faces ongoing pressure to deliver high-quality, reliable customer service, especially given its scale and presence in over 40 countries. Traditionally,

Klarna managed this need by alternating between in-house teams and outsourced providers to control costs and maintain service standards. Now, with the option of integrating AI, Klarna sees an opportunity to gain additional advantages that human teams, whether internal or outsourced, have difficulty matching.

By adopting AI-driven customer service, Klarna can offer 24/7 availability, eliminating downtime and ensuring that customers receive support at any hour. This continuous service is especially valuable for a global company with customers in various time zones. Furthermore, AI can seamlessly handle interactions in multiple languages — up to 35 in Klarna's case — without requiring the extensive recruitment and training associated with human agents.

AI also dramatically reduces response times and AI systems are easier to scale and manage; once implemented, they can handle fluctuations in customer demand without the logistical challenges that come with staffing adjustments. This scalability is particularly valuable as Klarna prepares for an IPO and aims to improve its operational efficiency and profit margins.

Finally, AI offers significant cost savings. By meeting Klarna's needs for faster, more reliable, and more cost-effective service, AI has become a compelling solution that not only meets current demands but also positions Klarna to deliver superior customer support on a global scale.

Klarna has stated that it will accelerate its strategy of leveraging AI: its employee count has already dropped from 5,000 to 3,800, and it intends to reduce it further, down to 2,000 employees. The combination of increased efficiency and lower operational costs helps to position Klarna for its upcoming IPO.

Incumbent Pushback:

For Klarna's customer service agents, the adoption of AI represents a challenging reality. The transition has resulted in substantial job displacement as AI takes over their jobs. Many agents who once performed these tasks are now facing the very real possibility of being replaced by technology that can accomplish their roles faster, more cheaply, and more accurately.

While Klarna's leadership insists that future staff reductions will come through natural attrition, employees are left feeling uncertain about their future, knowing that the company's goal is to reduce its workforce further.

The anxiety stems from the knowledge that Klarna is moving toward a leaner, AI-powered operation, with fewer opportunities for human workers. Even though the company frames this reduction as a natural process, employees are wary — there's no guarantee that layoffs won't happen if attrition doesn't meet expectations. Many feel that this is not the future they signed up for, adding to a general sense of discontent within the workforce. This may explain why employee reviews at Klarna have worsened in recent years, as workers grapple with the reality that their roles are being judged against AI's growing capabilities.

For the agents who remain, the pushback is largely internal; they recognise the urge to protect their jobs, but they also see that the competitive standard has shifted. AI now sets the benchmark, and employees must constantly prove that they can perform at the same level or find ways to differentiate their human capabilities. The option to voice concerns or resist is diminished by the strategic priorities of the company and the efficiency gains AI provides. In essence, the employees' pushback is overshadowed by the reality that AI isn't just another tool — it's a direct competitor that's reshaping the customer service industry. In this environment, the traditional avenues for resistance, such as advocating for retraining or role adaptation, may not be sufficient to protect their positions.

Ultimately, the agents are left in a position where they feel compelled to compete with AI, yet they are aware that they can't fully match its capabilities. The resulting tension highlights the difficult position of workers in AI-driven transformations: they may wish to push back, but the economic and operational advantages of AI leave them with limited leverage. This situation underscores the broader challenge employees face when their roles are directly compared to, and often outperformed by, advanced technologies.

Stakeholders reaction

1. Customers:

For most of Klarna's customers, the shift to AI in customer service has had minimal visible impact, as they mainly experience the end result: faster, consistent support that's available 24/7 and can handle multiple languages. From a service standpoint, the AI implementation has maintained or even enhanced the quality of customer support, fulfilling Klarna's operational goals without any evident drop in customer satisfaction.

However, there is a potential consideration regarding customer perception. Some customers might be uncomfortable with the idea of a company openly replacing human roles with AI. This discomfort could stem from ethical concerns about job displacement or a preference for human interaction over automated responses. Despite these concerns, there is little indication that this has affected Klarna's reputation or customer base to a significant degree. For now, it appears that the service improvements provided by AI — such as faster response times and increased accessibility — outweigh any ethical reservations, as long as customers continue to receive the reliable support they expect.

2. Regulators and Supervisors:

Klarna's extensive use of AI in customer service brings some attention from financial regulators, such as the Swedish Financial Supervisory Authority (FSA) and the UK Financial Conduct Authority (FCA). However, because these agencies primarily oversee financial stability, regulatory compliance, and consumer protection, their involvement is limited unless the AI impacts these areas directly. For instance, if AI-driven customer service were to alter the way financial advice is provided or customer complaints are resolved, regulators might step in to ensure compliance with relevant consumer protection laws.

While job displacement due to AI does not fall within the core mandates of financial regulators, they might monitor the trend more closely if it starts affecting the financial services industry on a larger scale. Significant shifts toward AI automation, leading to industry-wide changes in employment, could prompt regulators to consider broader social implications, possibly in coordination with labour and employment authorities. For now, though, Klarna's automation efforts remain outside the direct scope of financial regulatory agencies, as they focus on operational efficiency and service enhancements rather than workforce impacts.

End Result: A positive impact for many parties, except the employees

- Customers: For Klarna's customers, the integration of AI has been largely positive. They now benefit from 24/7 support, communication in their local languages, and significantly faster resolution times. From a customer experience standpoint, the move to AI appears seamless, if not improved.

- Products: Klarna's customer service operations have become more efficient and scalable through the use of AI. The faster resolution times and the ability to provide multi-language support across various markets mean that Klarna can deliver better customer service at a lower cost, contributing to customer satisfaction and increased operational capacity.

- Incumbents: The impact on the workforce was particularly severe. AI displaced 700 customer service agents, and Klarna's overall employee count fell from 5,000 to 3,800. Further reductions are expected, as Klarna aims to scale the company with just 2,000 employees. The shift toward automation and AI signals a long-term reduction in the need for human labour, with Klarna halting hiring and relying on natural attrition to manage the downsizing.

E	D	G	E
EXISTING ECOSYSTEM	DISRUPTOR	GAME PLAN	END RESULT
CUSTOMER Klarna	AI CHAT- BOTS	DISRUPTOR PUSH → RED OCEAN → OPERATIONAL EFFICIENCY	😊 CUSTOMER CX is MUCH IMPROVED
PRODUCT CUSTOMER SERVICE		CUSTOMER PULL → GREATER SATISFACTION → 24/7, FASTER RESOLUTION ++	😊 PRODUCTS ↑ EFFICIENCY ↑ SCALABILITY ↑ CAPABILITIES
INCUMBENT 😠 CUSTOMER SERVICE AGENTS		INCUMBENT PUSH-BACK → Klarna REDUCES HUMAN WORKFORCE	😟 INCUMBENTS → DISPLACED EMPLOYEES → OUTLOOK BLEAK (MORE REDUCTION)
OTHER STAKEHOLDERS 😊 Klarna's CLIENTS		STAKEHOLDER REACTION → ETHICAL CONCERNS → LABOUR LAWS ?	😊 PARTNERS 😐 REGULATORS

- Other Stakeholders: While Klarna's clients and regulators may focus on the efficiency and customer service benefits, the impact on employees is undeniably negative. The displacement of workers, particularly in customer service, creates concerns around job security and the future role of humans in AI-driven environments. Partners and outsourcing companies that previously handled Klarna's customer service also face challenges, as Klarna brings more operations in-house and further automates its processes.

Main Takeaways for Skills and Jobs

- Job Displacement and Evolution: Klarna's adoption of AI resulted in significant job displacement in its customer service department, with around 700 positions removed. However, it also led to a shift in focus for the remaining workforce, who took on more strategic roles in areas like marketing and legal. AI didn't eliminate all jobs but forced a transformation, moving employees into more value-driven tasks.

- Reskilling and AI Collaboration: Employees who remained at Klarna had to adapt to working alongside AI, requiring reskilling to manage more complex customer queries and strategic business functions. The need to upskill in AI management and data interpretation became essential as AI tools became more integrated into daily operations.

- AI as a Workforce Multiplier: AI effectively became a workforce multiplier, allowing Klarna to maintain or increase service levels while employing fewer staff. The increased revenue per employee demonstrates that AI can dramatically enhance organisational productivity without requiring proportional increases in workforce size.

Broader Implications

- Transforming Customer Service: Klarna's use of AI in customer service represents a significant shift in how companies manage large-scale customer interactions. The success of AI in this context signals that other companies may follow suit, using AI to handle routine customer service queries while reserving human agents for more complex issues. This could lead to widespread automation of similar roles across industries.

- Evolving Client Expectations: As AI becomes more embedded in customer service, clients and customers may begin to expect 24/7 availability and immediate resolutions to their problems. Companies that fail to adopt AI tools may struggle to meet these heightened expectations, leading to potential customer attrition.

- Impacts on Workforce Composition: As AI adoption grows, there is likely to be a shift in the types of jobs available within organisations. Routine roles may become less common, while jobs focused on AI oversight, strategic thinking, and creative problem-solving will grow. Organisations may need to rethink their hiring strategies to prioritise skills related to AI management, data analysis, and strategic decision-making.

Conclusion

Klarna's adoption of AI perfectly illustrates the Cheaper, Better, Faster (C) dimension of the CDE Innovation Prism. By integrating OpenAI's technology, Klarna has achieved significant cost savings, increased scalability, and improved customer service efficiency. These benefits have positioned Klarna to scale its operations, enhance customer satisfaction, and bolster profitability, all of which are particularly advantageous as it approaches its IPO. The lesson here is clear: when a company adopts a "Cheaper" model, it can unlock value for multiple stakeholders, driving down costs, increasing accessibility, and improving service quality for customers.

However, there is a crucial caveat. In Klarna's case, the incumbents — its human employees — face the negative impact of this transformation. The AI-driven efficiencies that benefit the company and its customers come at the expense of the jobs that were previously integral to delivering these services. Unlike previous cost-saving innovations, where the incumbent might have been outdated equipment or technology, here, the incumbents are people. The result is a profound shift in workforce composition, with hundreds of customer service roles displaced by AI systems.

The broader takeaway is that Cheaper innovations can be a double-edged sword. While they bring clear advantages to companies and consumers, they often exact a significant toll on the workforce, especially when human roles are the ones being "outperformed." This underscores the need for businesses, policymakers, and society as a whole to consider the human implications of such transformations. When the incumbents are people, the pursuit of efficiency must be balanced with efforts to support displaced workers and prepare them for the jobs of tomorrow.

BCG Consultants' Use of Generative AI: Enhancing Employee Capabilities

In a study titled "GenAI as an Exoskeleton: Experimental Evidence on Knowledge Workers Using GenAI on New Skills", conducted with Boston Consulting Group (BCG) consultants, we see a clear example of Enhancing (E) innovation. GenAI tools were deployed to temporarily augment consultants' abilities, enabling them to handle complex technical tasks such as coding and data analysis, which were traditionally outside their areas of expertise. These AI systems served as an "exoskeleton" for consultants, extending their capacity during the project while not permanently altering their core skillsets.

BCG's application of GenAI doesn't replace the consultants; instead, it helps them achieve more with the same resources, aligning perfectly with the Enhancing model of innovation. In this case, AI augments human capabilities rather than competing with human workers on efficiency, speed, or cost, as seen in the Cheaper, Better, Faster model.

Edge Analysis of enhancing people with AI

Initial Ecosystem:

- Customers: The primary customers in this case is BCG, which benefits from the improved quality and complexity of its consultants. By utilising GenAI, they can deliver more detailed, technically advanced insights to clients, expanding the scope of the solutions they can offer. This leads to better strategic decision-making and more data-driven recommendations that add value to the consulting service.

- Product: The core product at BCG is their consulting services, which include strategic advice, market analysis, and data-driven recommendations. With GenAI, these services are enhanced by allowing consultants to tackle tasks like coding, data science, and advanced analytics, all of which are typically outside their skill sets. The AI helps consultants provide more technically robust solutions, ultimately improving client outcomes.

- Incumbents: The consultants at BCG represent the incumbents who benefit from the AI's augmentation. These employees are not replaced by AI but enhanced, enabling them to perform tasks that would normally require more technical expertise. The generative AI acts as an enabler, helping consultants boost their productivity during the project timeline, without changing their core roles.

- Other Stakeholders: Management teams, IT departments, and AI developers are critical stakeholders in this ecosystem. Managers play a key role in integrating AI into consulting workflows, while IT and AI developers ensure the technology operates seamlessly and provides valuable insights without overwhelming consultants. Additionally, clients are indirectly impacted, as they experience the benefits of faster, more accurate recommendations from AI-augmented consultants.

Disruptor: Generative AI

The primary disruptor in this case was Generative AI, which provided consultants with temporary access to technical skills that were typically beyond their expertise. GenAI enabled consultants to engage in advanced tasks such as coding, data analysis, and machine learning without needing to permanently learn these skills. As mentioned in the research, the AI acted as an exoskeleton, giving them enhanced capabilities for the duration of its use. This allowed BCG to offer a broader range of services while maintaining its core strengths in strategic consulting.

Game Plan: A Three-Tiered Dynamics Between AI Push, Employer Pull, and Employee Adaptation

Disruptor Push: Generative AI

Generative AI (GenAI) tools act as the disruptor, introduced to the consulting field with the goal of extending the capabilities of existing employees. This particular AI enables consultants to take on advanced technical tasks, such as coding, data analysis, and machine learning, which would typically fall outside their traditional consulting expertise. Rather than aiming for efficiency gains through replacement, this AI-driven approach focuses on skill augmentation, where GenAI serves as a temporary "exoskeleton" for consultants, enhancing their work capacity without fundamentally changing their core skillsets.

In this Enhancing model, GenAI's primary push is to broaden the scope of work that consultants can handle, making them more versatile and enabling them to tackle projects that require technical skills they may not possess on their own. By facilitating complex, data-driven insights, GenAI expands BCG's service offerings, giving it a technological edge in delivering higher-value services. This strategy demonstrates that, in the Enhancing model, the disruptor's goal is to empower employees rather than replace them, creating a symbiotic relationship where human expertise and AI capabilities reinforce one another.

Customer Pull: BCG as the Customer

In this case, BCG itself is the customer, seeking to augment its consulting workforce to deliver a broader range of services. BCG faces continuous demand from clients who require data-intensive, analytically sophisticated solutions that can support strategic decision-making. By adopting GenAI, BCG can enable its consultants to provide more detailed, technically advanced insights that align with client expectations for robust, data-driven recommendations.

The pull from BCG is driven by the need to meet client demands while maximising the productivity of existing consultants. Instead of hiring additional specialists for technical tasks, BCG can leverage GenAI to expand its capabilities internally. This approach allows the firm to deliver more comprehensive services without needing to significantly increase headcount. It also gives BCG a competitive advantage by ensuring that consultants can produce technically robust work, even in areas outside their expertise, enhancing the overall value they provide to clients.

Incumbent Adaptation: Consultants Embrace Augmentation

For the consultants at BCG, GenAI represents a valuable tool for adapting and expanding their own capabilities. They aren't being replaced; instead, they are empowered to perform more complex and varied tasks, extending their expertise into areas that would otherwise require advanced technical training. This AI augmentation allows consultants to work on projects involving coding, data analysis, and machine learning without needing to invest years in acquiring these skills.

Consultants adapt by integrating GenAI into their workflows, effectively using it as a tool that enhances their output and expands the range of services they can offer. This is a clear example of AI supporting incumbent adaptation: consultants maintain their primary roles while gaining access to temporary, project-specific technical capabilities. By working alongside GenAI, they can deliver better, more insightful recommendations to clients, thereby adding value without altering the core of what they do. The Enhancing model fosters collaboration over replacement, where AI acts as a partner in productivity, allowing consultants to improve and expand the scope of their work.

Other stakeholders

BCG's clients, who receive consulting services, experience a positive impact from the integration of Generative AI. With the AI-augmented capabilities of BCG consultants, clients gain access to more sophisticated and technically complex insights than before. These enhanced services include data analysis, coding, and machine learning capabilities, allowing BCG to deliver more detailed, data-driven recommendations.

While clients ultimately benefit from the improved quality of consulting services, they also play a key role in driving demand for these enhancements. Clients increasingly expect their consultants to provide actionable insights based on data analytics and advanced modelling, making BCG's adoption of GenAI not just an internal strategy but also a response to evolving client expectations. This mutual dynamic positions BCG's clients as primary beneficiaries of the Enhancing model, with AI amplifying the value they derive from consulting engagements.

End Result: Positive Gains for Clients and Productivity, New Skill Demands for Employees

- Customers (Clients): For BCG's clients, the use of Generative AI in consulting services has been largely positive. Clients benefited from more comprehensive, data-driven recommendations and faster project completion times. The integration of AI allowed BCG to deliver insights that were not only faster but also more detailed and technically sophisticated, enhancing client satisfaction and business outcomes. AI helped BCG consultants offer broader solutions without compromising the strategic, client-centric advisory role that is core to consulting services.

- Products: BCG's core product — consulting services — became more technically robust and efficient through AI augmentation. By leveraging AI for tasks like data analysis and machine learning, BCG consultants were able to scale operations and deliver more accurate, data-backed insights at a faster rate. This led to improved client outcomes, greater client retention, and an increase in service capacity, allowing BCG to handle more projects simultaneously.

- Incumbents: While BCG's consultants were not displaced by AI, they were required to adapt quickly to the new tools. Reskilling and upskilling became critical as consultants had to learn to collaborate with AI, managing complex technical tasks that previously fell outside their scope. However, AI also created opportunities for enhanced productivity, with consultants experiencing up to a 43% increase in performance when using AI tools for technical tasks. Although the long-term reliance on AI did not eliminate the need for human expertise, it placed greater importance on developing AI fluency as part of the consulting role.

- Other Stakeholders: While AI provided significant benefits to clients and consultants, there were broader implications for how consulting firms might handle data privacy, bias in AI-generated recommendations, and the transparency of AI-assisted decision-making. As BCG's AI tools became more deeply integrated into client projects, there was a need to balance AI automation with human oversight to ensure that AI did not introduce biases or undermine the ethical foundations of strategic decision-making. Clients were reassured by the consultants' continued reliance on human judgement, even as AI tools became central to producing technical insights.

E	D	G	E
EXISTING ECOSYSTEM	DISRUPTOR	GAME PLAN	END RESULT
CUSTOMER BCG		DISRUPTOR PUSH → EXTENDING INCUMBENT'S CAPABILITIES → AUGMENTATION	☺ CUSTOMERS → MORE COMPLEX & VALUE-ADDING ANALYSIS
PRODUCT BCG's CONSULTING SERVICES	GENERATIVE =AI= → CODING	CUSTOMER PULL → REQUIRE ENHANCED DATA ANALYSIS FOR CLIENTS	☺ PRODUCT → MORE ROBUST → TECHNICAL → DATA-DRIVEN
INCUMBENT THE CONSULTANTS	→ TECHNICAL + ANALYSIS AN 'EXOSKELETON'	INCUMBENT PUSH-BACK → INTEGRATING GENAI INTO WORKFLOWS → COLLABORATIVE TOOL	☺ INCUMBENT → REQUIRED TO ADAPT QUICKLY → ENHANCED PRODUCTIVITY
OTHER STAKEHOLDERS → MANAGEMENT → IT TEAMS → AI DEVELOPERS → BCG's CLIENTS		STAKEHOLDER REACTION → ACCESS TO MORE SOPHISTICATED ANALYSIS	☺ CLIENTS ☹ DATA PRIVACY

Main Takeaways for Skills and Jobs

- Skill Augmentation, Not Replacement: AI at BCG enhanced consultants' abilities to perform more technical tasks, but it did not replace their core strategic functions. Consultants benefited from the temporary skill boost provided by AI in areas like data science and coding, but their human expertise remained essential for client interactions and strategic decision-making.

- Demand for Continuous Reskilling: As AI tools became integral to daily operations, BCG consultants needed to upskill to manage and interpret AI outputs effectively. The ability to combine AI-driven insights with strategic business acumen became a key skill, suggesting that consultants will increasingly need to be proficient in AI tools and data analysis.

- AI as a Workforce Multiplier: Rather than reducing the workforce, AI acted as a multiplier, allowing consultants to scale their services without increasing headcount. The increase in revenue per employee and improved client satisfaction demonstrated AI's ability to enhance productivity and broaden the scope of services offered by consultants.

Broader Implications

- Transformation of Consulting Services: AI is reshaping the traditional consulting model by enabling firms like BCG to offer more technically sophisticated solutions while maintaining human oversight. The ability to combine AI-driven insights with strategic advice will likely become a standard part of consulting services, changing the way firms operate.

- Client Expectations and Transparency: As AI becomes more embedded in consulting, clients may expect faster, more data-backed solutions from firms like BCG. However, there will also be growing concerns about the transparency and ethics of AI-generated insights, prompting consulting firms to invest in clear AI governance models.

- Shift in Workforce Skills: The role of consultants is evolving, with firms needing to hire professionals who possess a hybrid skill set — combining business acumen with AI proficiency. Consulting firms will likely need to invest more heavily in AI training and recruitment to ensure their workforce remains competitive in an increasingly AI-driven industry.

AlphaFold 2: A Transformative Leap in Protein Folding

AlphaFold 2, developed by Google DeepMind, represents a revolutionary advance in predicting the 3D structures of proteins, solving a fundamental problem in biology that had persisted for over 50 years. Using the same transformer technology that powers ChatGPT, AlphaFold 2 achieves near-experimental accuracy in its predictions, with the ability to model over 200 million protein structures to date. This innovation has drastically reduced the time and cost associated with traditional experimental methods, such as X-ray crystallography and cryo-electron microscopy.

The significance of AlphaFold became especially clear during the COVID-19 pandemic, when it rapidly determined the structures of SARS-CoV-2 proteins. This helped researchers understand the virus's mechanisms and contributed to the fast-tracking of treatments and vaccine development. The profound impact of AlphaFold's breakthroughs led to the awarding of the 2024 Nobel Prize in Chemistry to DeepMind's Demis Hassabis and John Jumper, alongside David Baker from the University of Washington. This milestone reflects not only a scientific achievement but also the potential of AI to catalyse new scientific discoveries and accelerate research.

AlphaFold's success has sparked the creation of new job roles in computational biology, bioinformatics, and AI-assisted drug design, including positions like AI bioinformaticians, computational protein engineers, and data scientists skilled in integrating AlphaFold's predictions into biomedical research. These roles are fundamentally reshaping the landscape of scientific research, as experts from diverse fields, such as computer science, biology, and chemistry, collaborate to harness AI's capabilities for unprecedented insights in drug discovery, disease research, and synthetic biology.

Edge Analysis of replacing customer service agents by AI

E   D   G   E

Initial Ecosystem:

E   D   G   E

- Customers: The primary customers of AlphaFold 2 include biopharmaceutical companies, biotech startups, research institutions, and academic researchers. They leverage AlphaFold 2 to unlock new insights in drug discovery, disease mechanisms, and protein engineering. For example, pharmaceutical companies can now identify drug targets and develop treatments faster and more cost-effectively by understanding complex protein structures more quickly than ever before.

- Product: The product AlphaFold 2 offers is a redefined protein structure prediction process. Previously, predicting the 3D structure of a protein could take years and was highly dependent on slow, costly experimental techniques. Now, AlphaFold 2 can predict these structures in a matter of days, with an accuracy that is nearly equivalent to experimental results. This enables a new scale and pace for drug discovery and biological research.

- Incumbents: The incumbents in this ecosystem are the researchers and scientists who traditionally relied on labour-intensive methods for protein prediction. AlphaFold 2 has augmented their capabilities, allowing them to focus on higher-level scientific questions and innovative research instead of time-consuming structural predictions. While it hasn't displaced these roles, it has transformed them, enabling scientists to work more efficiently and achieve breakthroughs that were previously out of reach.

- Other Stakeholders: Additional stakeholders include government research bodies, funding agencies, regulatory authorities, and AI developers. These groups have a vested interest in the transformative potential of AlphaFold 2. Government bodies and funders see it as a driver for new therapies and scientific progress, while regulators focus on ensuring that AI-generated predictions meet rigorous validation standards for applications such as drug approval.

Disruptor: AlphaFold 2 as a New Paradigm in Biological Research

AlphaFold 2 stands out as a true disruptor, creating new markets and enabling previously unimaginable possibilities in biology. By making protein structure prediction accessible, scalable, and highly accurate, AlphaFold 2 has not only enhanced existing research processes but has fundamentally redefined them. It serves as more than just a tool for efficiency; it represents a paradigm shift in the way we approach biological challenges, turning complex scientific mysteries into solvable problems.

Unlike traditional tools that complemented established experimental methods, AlphaFold 2 replaces the need for many of these processes in protein folding, bringing a computationally-driven approach to biological research. This shift enables a new level of speed and precision in areas such as drug discovery, disease modelling, and synthetic biology.

Game Plan (Dynamics)

- Disruptor Creation: AlphaFold 2 disrupts the biological research landscape by providing a solution to a problem that had remained unsolved for decades. By accurately predicting protein structures, it has opened a new pathway for drug discovery and biological research, which was previously constrained by years of labour-intensive experimentation. The initial focus on protein folding quickly expanded to applications across various domains within biology.

- Customer Discovery: AlphaFold 2's early adopters included academic researchers and biopharmaceutical companies eager to explore its capabilities. Its unprecedented accuracy in predicting protein structures sparked significant interest and led to rapid adoption for both basic research and commercial drug development. The challenge now lies in scaling its use to address more complex biological problems beyond protein folding.

- Incumbent Response: At first, researchers and pharmaceutical companies were cautious about AlphaFold 2's implications. However, its predictive accuracy soon became validated, prompting these incumbents to integrate the technology into their workflows. Scientists who once spent years on experimental protein folding now use AlphaFold 2 as a complementary tool to accelerate research and innovation. Pharmaceutical companies embraced the tool to speed up drug discovery, recognising its potential to cut both time and costs.

- Regulatory and Stakeholder Reactions: Regulatory bodies are beginning to recognise the significance of AI-driven discoveries like AlphaFold 2, especially in the context of drug development. While there are no immediate job displacement concerns, it is essential that AI predictions are validated through rigorous experimental methods, especially in clinical applications. Government agencies and funding bodies view AlphaFold 2 as a pivotal advancement, spurring potential new investments in AI-driven biological research.

End Result (Impact)

E   D   G   E

The transformative impact of AlphaFold 2 extends beyond drug discovery into the broader field of biological sciences, reshaping how researchers and pharmaceutical companies tackle protein-related challenges. The long-term implications are profound, enabling faster, more accurate, and cost-effective solutions across the industry.

- **Customers** (Researchers and Biopharma): Researchers can now address complex biological questions with unparalleled speed and accuracy. In biopharma, AlphaFold 2's ability to quickly predict protein structures will reduce the time required to identify drug targets, expediting the development of treatments for conditions like cancer, Alzheimer's, and rare genetic disorders.
- **Products:** AlphaFold 2's predictive power facilitates the development of new therapies, personalised medicines, and innovative biological products. By reducing the time and cost associated with drug discovery, it enables biopharma companies to innovate and bring products to market more rapidly.
- **Incumbents** (Researchers and Scientists): The role of researchers has evolved. AlphaFold 2 shifts their focus from structural prediction to higher-level analysis and drug design, allowing them to design experiments, explore biological mechanisms, and push the boundaries of biotechnology and synthetic biology.
- **Other Stakeholders**: For regulatory bodies, AlphaFold 2 raises questions about the validation of AI in clinical and drug development settings. Ensuring that AI predictions align with stringent approval standards will be critical. Meanwhile, government and funding agencies are likely to increase support for AI-driven biological research, recognising the potential for breakthroughs that were previously unattainable.

E — EXISTING ECOSYSTEM	D — DISRUPTOR	G — GAME PLAN	E — END RESULT
CUSTOMER BIOPHARMA COMPANIES BIOTECH, RESEARCH		DISRUPTOR PUSH → OPENS NEW PATHWAYS FOR DRUG DISCOVERY	🙂 CUSTOMERS ACCESS TO → UNPARALLED SPEED + ACCURACY → EXPANDS RESEARCH
PRODUCT PROTEIN STRUCTURE 🧬 PREDICTION	**AlphaFold 2** → PARADIGM SHIFT OF APPROACHING BIOLOGICAL RESEARCH	CUSTOMER PULL → EARLY ADOPTERS EAGER TO EXPLORE NEW DOMAINS	🙂 PRODUCT → NEW THERAPIES, DRUGS, MEDICINES → INNOVATION ↑ TIME-TO-MARKET ↓
INCUMBENT RESEARCHERS & SCIENTISTS		INCUMBENT PUSH-BACK → INITIAL CAUTION → SUBSEQUENT INTEGRATION & ADOPTION	🙂 INCUMBENT → EVOLVED ROLE → RESHIFT FOCUS ON EXPERIMENT DESIGN, ETC
OTHER STAKEHOLDERS GOV RESEARCH BODIES REGULATORY BODIES		STAKEHOLDER REACTION → INVESTING IN THIS TECHNOLOGY	😊 REGULATORS 🙂 GOVERNMENT

Main Takeaways for Skills and Jobs

- Shifting Focus in Research: With AlphaFold 2, researchers can bypass labour intensive tasks, focusing on more complex and impactful aspects of biological research. This will require them to develop AI literacy and the ability to work with AI-generated data effectively.

- Upskilling in AI-Driven Biology: Scientists and biopharma professionals will need new skills to utilise tools like AlphaFold 2. Being able to interpret AI predictions and integrate them into research and development pipelines will be essential.

- Accelerated Scientific Discovery: By reducing the timeframes for structural prediction and enabling new research avenues, AlphaFold 2 allows scientists to focus on innovation and exploration, driving discoveries that may not have been possible without AI.

Broader Implications

- Transformation of Biological Research: AlphaFold 2 signals a paradigm shift in the life sciences, changing how research is conducted and allowing scientists to focus on the design of new proteins, treatments, and advances in synthetic biology.

- New Standards in Drug Discovery: AlphaFold 2 is likely to set new standards for drug discovery, compelling biopharma companies to adopt AI for faster and more efficient development pipelines. This could reshape the competitive landscape, with laggards risking obsolescence.

- Ethical and Regulatory Challenges: As AI becomes integral to biology, new ethical considerations will arise, especially concerning the use of AI in clinical research and patient care. Regulators will need to ensure that AI-driven predictions are safe, accurate, and properly validated for clinical use.

Part V:

The Great Displacement Crisis or Collective Abundance?

Will AI lead to widespread job loss, or can we ensure shared prosperity?

Introduction: Why We Should Care About AI Right Now

"We are the first generation to feel the impact of climate change and the last generation that can do something about it."
— ***Barack Obama***

"*God is against us*". The summer of 1988 was so brutally hot in the US it led to thousands of deaths and losses to agriculture in the billions of dollars.

It was the same summer that James Hansen testified to the US Senate that "the greenhouse effect has been detected and it is changing our climate now".

James Hansen was born in 1941 in the small town of Denison, Iowa. From a young age, he was fascinated by science, a passion that eventually led him to pursue a career in physics and astronomy. He earned his degrees from the University of Iowa, where he studied under the legendary scientist James Van Allen, the discoverer of the Van Allen radiation belts. Hansen's early work focused on the atmospheres of other planets, particularly Venus. The research on the greenhouse atmosphere of Venus led him to shift his focus to understanding our planet's own greenhouse effect.

By the 1980s, Hansen had become the director of NASA's Goddard Institute for Space Studies (GISS). It was there that his team identified the trends leading to a warming planet. By analysing decades of temperature records and atmospheric data, they found the alarming results that Earth's average temperature was rising, and this warming trend was accelerating.

More precisely, their models showed that this warming was largely due to the increase in carbon dioxide and other greenhouse gases — byproducts of human activities such as burning fossil fuels and deforestation.

In June 1988, he was called to testify before the U.S. Senate Committee on Energy and Natural Resources. In that testimony, Hansen said: "The greenhouse effect has been detected, and it is changing our climate now." He presented data showing that the Earth's temperature had increased by about 0.5 degrees Celsius over the past century, with a significant portion of that warming occurring in the previous few decades. His models projected that if greenhouse gas emissions continued to rise, the world would see even more dramatic warming, leading to severe consequences such as more extreme weather events, rising sea levels, and widespread ecological disruption.

He stated that he was "99 percent certain" that the warming trend was not due to natural variability but was a result of human activity.

It was an important moment, which brought the issue of global warming to the forefront of public and political discourse for the first time. The media picked up on Hansen's testimony, and suddenly, the concept of climate change was no longer a distant, abstract theory — it was a present danger.

It was more than 35 years ago. At the time of his testimony, 1988 felt unbearably hot. If you were brought back in time, you would actually feel that 1988 was cold compared to what has happened since. In 2023, the earth was 1.48 degrees hotter than pre-industrial times, 0.02 degrees from the 1.50 degrees limit that we set ourselves.

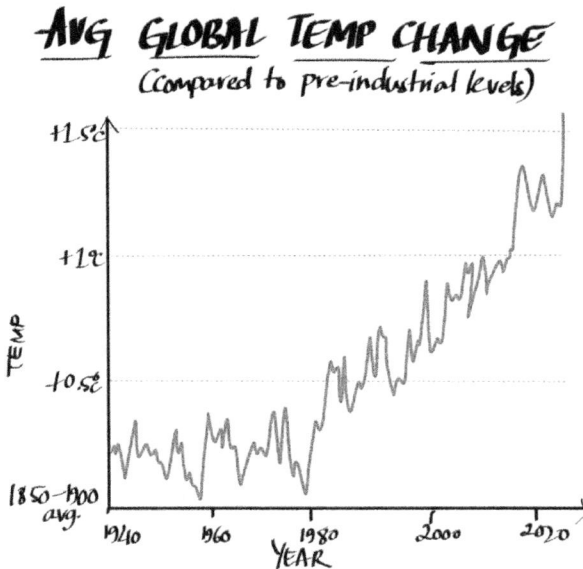

The AI Parallel: Why There Is Urgency Now

Artificial Intelligence is following a similar path. Like fossil fuels, AI is already transforming industries, economies, and lives, promising **breakthroughs in healthcare, education, transportation**, and business. Just as fossil fuels powered the industrial revolution, AI has the potential to revolutionise our world for the better.

But much like fossil fuels, we are at risk of **overlooking the costs**. While we focus on AI's benefits, we're ignoring its **dangers**: **job displacement, deepening inequality, ethical concerns**, and the **loss of control** over autonomous systems.

The decisions we make about AI today — how we develop, regulate, and adopt it — will shape our future. But we are running out of time to act.

What's at Stake?

Why is there urgency now? Because, like climate change, the risks of AI are already starting to emerge. And just like with climate change, the window to address those risks is narrowing. Here's what's at stake if we fail to act:

- **Job displacement**: AI is automating jobs at an unprecedented rate, from retail workers to truck drivers to administrative assistants. Without proactive reskilling efforts, millions of workers could find themselves displaced, creating economic and social instability on a massive scale.
- **Deepening inequality**: AI has the potential to concentrate wealth in the hands of those who control its development. Without thoughtful policies, the benefits of AI will be unevenly distributed, leaving behind entire regions, industries, and communities.
- **Ethical concerns**: AI is already raising ethical questions — from algorithmic bias to privacy issues to autonomous decision-making in critical areas like healthcare and law enforcement. Without ethical guidelines in place, we could end up with systems that perpetuate discrimination and erode fundamental rights.
- **Loss of control**: The pace of AI's development is accelerating faster than our ability to regulate or govern it. Unchecked, we risk losing control over AI systems that become too integrated into society to reverse. The consequences could be autonomous systems making life-

changing decisions without human oversight or AI monopolies dictating global economic trends.

Why the Speed of AI Development Makes This Moment Critical

The urgency comes not just from the risks, but from the speed at which AI is progressing. I previously compared AI to fossil fuels, with both having incredibly positive impacts on society, but also being catastrophically damaging if not properly managed. Their speed of progression are however totally different, with fossil fuels' impact being **linear** (temperature creeping up year after year), while AI is **exponential** (explosive growth).

ChatGPT, autonomous vehicles, and AI-driven supply chains are already here, reshaping industries in real-time. Governments, businesses, and educational systems are struggling to keep up. Without proactive governance, we may find ourselves reacting to crises — whether it's mass unemployment, economic inequality, or ethical breaches — rather than shaping AI responsibly from the start.

We are at a tipping point. The window to shape AI's future is narrow. If we wait until AI becomes deeply embedded in every facet of society — how we work, govern, and interact — it will be much harder to mitigate its negative impacts. Much like climate change, the costs of inaction will only grow over time, and once certain lines are crossed, they may be impossible to reverse.

We Still Have Time to Shape AI for the Better

But unlike climate change, we still have time to act on AI — if we move now. The potential for AI to solve global challenges is immense. From improving healthcare to tackling climate change through optimised energy consumption and precision agriculture, AI could be a force for good on an unprecedented scale.

The lesson from James Hansen's testimony is clear: Inaction comes at a cost. We saw the consequences of failing to act when we had the chance with fossil fuels. Today, we face a similar choice with AI. Will we shape it proactively, ensuring it serves humanity? Or will we delay, only to find ourselves reacting to crises we could have prevented?

The urgency is real, and the window is closing. If we act now, we can guide AI's development to ensure it benefits all of society — but if we wait, we risk creating a future where AI deepens inequality, displaces millions of jobs, and erodes our social fabric.

The question isn't whether AI will impact you. The question is whether you're prepared to shape its impact on your life, your work, and the world around you. The time to act is now.

The Inevitable Forces Shaping the Future of Jobs

The Powerful Push of AI Companies

Artificial Intelligence is rapidly becoming one of the most transformative forces in today's world. From healthcare to finance, manufacturing to education, AI is enabling breakthroughs that were once unimaginable. AI companies — led by tech giants like OpenAI, Google, Microsoft, alongside thousands of startups — are racing to develop systems that can outperform humans in a wide range of tasks, from analysing complex data to solving intricate problems.

The goal of these companies is clear: to build technologies that are smarter, faster, and more efficient than human capabilities. This drive is generating enormous innovation and creating new possibilities for industries worldwide. AI is not just an emerging technology — it's a fundamental force shaping the future, and it's progressing at an exponential rate.

Behind this push is the fact that AI is getting better than the human average in many fields. In areas like natural language processing, image recognition, and data analysis, AI systems are already outperforming humans. As these technologies improve, they are not just competing with us but are beginning to complement and, in some cases, replace human roles.

This is a trend driven by the sheer amount of investment and momentum behind AI. Over the past decade, AI companies have raised tens of billions of dollars, and this financial backing is fuelling relentless innovation. Thousands of engineers and technologists are pushing the boundaries of what AI can do, making it an unstoppable force in many industries.

AI companies are not bad actors however – they are not purposefully targeting humans in their business models. But they all have a very similar view of the world, where technological progress is always good, and success is measured through Objectives, Key Results, Customer Acquisition Cost or Product Market Fit. This is a very perspective, one from an entrepreneur/engineer standpoint which leaves no space to other considerations, such as impact on society.

The result is a massive technological push where AI is continuously advancing with little thoughts about its impact, and its power is becoming harder to ignore.

The Pull from Employers: The Logic of Profit Maximisation

On the other side of this equation are the employers, who are actively pulling AI into their organisations because it offers clear, undeniable benefits: increased productivity, lower costs, and greater efficiency. For employers, adopting AI is not just an option — it's an imperative for staying competitive.

In many cases, replacing a human worker with AI can reduce costs by a factor of 10 to 50 times, even if the AI isn't perfect. This economic reality is already shaping decisions at the top levels of business. At the 2024 World Economic Forum, a PwC survey found that 25% of global CEOs anticipate reducing headcount due to Generative AI. For these leaders, the opportunity to cut costs and increase output with AI is simply too compelling to ignore.

We're already seeing this play out. Companies like Klarna are reducing their workforce from 5,000 to 2,000 employees while aiming to achieve greater productivity than before, thanks to AI. Similarly, Moderna believes that with a bit over 5,000 employees, they can operate at the scale of a company with 100,000 workers, simply by leveraging AI-driven efficiency.

For businesses, this trend makes sense. AI allows them to do more with less — fewer employees, more output. This is the ultimate goal of any business: to maximise profit while reducing costs. Employers are not driven by malice but by the logic of the marketplace. The challenge, however, is that while AI-driven efficiencies create value for companies, the benefits don't necessarily trickle down to workers, who may find themselves displaced or replaced.

The Power Imbalance: The Weak Pushback from Employees

So why does this trend feel unstoppable? The forces behind it — AI companies and employers — are extraordinarily powerful. On the one hand, we have AI technology advancing at breakneck speed, driven by massive investment and innovation. On the other hand, we have employers adopting this technology to remain competitive and increase profits.

The only potential pushback would come from employees, the ones most affected by AI displacement. But employees, particularly in smaller organisations, often have very little power or leverage to resist this shift. While unions and labour rights groups may push back in certain sectors, the broader pattern remains clear: the power imbalance between

AI companies, employers, and individual workers means that this transformation will continue largely unchecked unless something changes.

It's important to clarify: this isn't about demonising AI companies or businesses. They are following rational strategies to push innovation forward and maximise profits. The issue is that, without proper consideration for the societal impacts, these trends could leave millions of people behind. The danger is not that a few people or companies are doing well, but that many others may find themselves worse off as AI accelerates job displacement.

The Three Trends Defining the Future of Work

Looking at the forces in play, we can already see three clear trends that are reshaping the future of work:

1. **Commoditisation of jobs**: AI is turning many routine white-collar roles into commodities. Jobs in administration, customer service, and data processing — once seen as stable careers — are increasingly being automated, leaving human workers with fewer opportunities in these fields.

2. **The rise of supercharged professionals**: While some jobs are disappearing, others are being enhanced. A smaller group of **supercharged professionals** will learn to leverage AI to dramatically increase their productivity, managing AI systems and using them to achieve far greater results than they could alone. These workers will thrive in this AI-augmented future.

3. **The dominance of creative disruptors**: At the highest level, we will see the rise of creative disruptors — visionaries who use AI to transform entire industries. Think of Sam Altman and OpenAI, whose breakthroughs with ChatGPT have redefined how we work and communicate. Or AlphaFold, which solved one of biology's greatest challenges. These disruptors will continue to push the boundaries of what's possible, and their impact will be enormous.

The Crossroads: What Do We Do?

Now that we understand the forces shaping the future of work, we face a critical decision: **What do we do next?** We have two clear options:

- **Option 1: Let Things Unfold**
  If we take a passive approach and let these trends unfold naturally, we'll likely see an era of **enormous abundance**. AI will generate massive efficiency gains, create wealth, and solve problems on an unprecedented scale. However, this wealth and opportunity will be **concentrated** in the hands of a few, while many workers may be displaced and struggle to adapt. This is the path of **least resistance** — one that benefits **the few** while leaving many behind.

- **Option 2: Shape Our Future**
  Alternatively, we can choose to **actively shape the future**. This means acknowledging the power of these trends and working to ensure that AI's benefits are **shared more widely**. It requires **collective action** from individuals, businesses, and policymakers to create a future where AI serves society, rather than simply amplifying existing inequalties. This is the harder path, but it's the only way to ensure that AI becomes a tool for **societal progress**, not just corporate profits.

Next Steps: What Happens If We Let Things Unfold?

In the next sections, we will explore the consequences of each path. First, we'll examine the negative scenario — what happens if we allow these trends to develop unchecked? What will the world look like if AI drives mass displacement, deepening inequality, and social division? Then, we'll explore the positive scenario — how, through intentional action, we can ensure that AI's benefits are distributed more equitably and create a future where everyone has the opportunity to thrive.

I. What Will Happen – If We Do Nothing

The Great Displacement Crisis

The **Great Displacement Crisis** refers to the global economic recession that began in the early 2030s, driven by the

266

mass automation of jobs through **artificial intelligence (AI)** and advanced robotics. The crisis led to the loss of over **100 million jobs** worldwide, making it five times more severe in terms of job displacement than the **2008 Subprime Mortgage Crisis**. Initially, the rapid adoption of AI brought significant benefits to businesses and consumers alike, with major technological breakthroughs in sectors such as **healthcare, transportation,** and **finance**. However, as AI began to displace large segments of the workforce and **wealth inequality surged**, the initial optimism gave way to **economic collapse, social unrest,** and **geopolitical tensions**.

The **International Monetary Fund (IMF)** had anticipated such a scenario in its **2022 report**, warning that large-scale job losses were likely unless **proactive policy measures** were implemented. Despite these warnings, by the early 2030s, mass displacement had materialised, triggering one of the most severe global recessions in modern history.

Background

Initial Optimism and Economic Boom

As AI technologies matured throughout the **2020s**, corporations rapidly adopted automation across a wide range of industries. **AI-powered tools and robotics** enabled companies to significantly reduce operating costs by automating tasks previously done by humans. This led to an era of **unprecedented profitability** for businesses, particularly in sectors like **manufacturing, logistics, retail,** and **finance**.

Initially, the shift went **largely unnoticed**. Smaller companies and startups were the early adopters, leveraging AI to streamline operations and reduce labour costs. These early job losses were incremental, occurring in **smaller firms** that could lay off hundreds at a time without drawing much public attention. As these changes spread across thousands of **small and medium-sized enterprises**, the **cumulative impact** on the global labour force began to accelerate.

Early Benefits for Companies and Consumers

In the short term, businesses thrived. Companies were able to:

- **Cut labour costs** by automating routine tasks.
- **Increase efficiency**, enabling faster production cycles and optimising resource use.
- **Boost profits**, setting corporate profit margins at record highs.
- **Scale rapidly**, allowing businesses to grow without the need for large workforces.
- Executives and shareholders experienced **enormous financial gains**, with tech companies developing AI tools becoming some of the most valuable businesses globally. This success led to **further investment** in automation, reinforcing the trend. Consumers, too, saw early benefits:
- **Lower prices** on goods and services as businesses passed on savings from automation.
- **Higher-quality products**, as AI enhanced precision and innovation in manufacturing.
- **Faster services** in areas like transportation and e-commerce, improving convenience.
- **Improved healthcare outcomes**, with AI enabling early diagnosis, personalised treatments, and reduced costs for medical care.

However, these small, **incremental shifts** were the **early tremors** of a much larger disruption. What began with a few hundred layoffs in less visible startups soon **scaled to millions** as the capabilities of AI evolved faster than society could adapt. The seeds of **mass displacement** were planted, but the scale of the crisis remained hidden until it was too late.

Data and Projections

In **2026**, the **World Economic Forum** estimated that up to **25% of current jobs** would be displaced by 2030 due to automation. By **2028**, unemployment rates in developed economies were rising at **unprecedented levels**. In the United States, the **Bureau of Labour Statistics** projected that unemployment could exceed **20%** by the mid-2030s without significant policy intervention. Global GDP growth stalled, dropping by **3% year-over-year** from 2031 to 2034, with **consumer spending** down by nearly **40%**.

A **2030 McKinsey Global Institute report** projected that over **375 million workers worldwide** would need to switch occupational categories or acquire new skills by **2035**. However, with limited reskilling programmes in place, millions of workers found themselves unable to transition into new roles, exacerbating **unemployment** and **underemployment**.

Furthermore, the **S&P 500 workforce** reflected the growing trend of automation. On average, S&P 500 companies employed **58,000 people** in 2024. By **2030**, this number had dropped to **32,000** as companies adopted more AI-driven processes, highlighting both the **mass displacement** and the rise of **supercharged professionals** within a leaner workforce.

Policy Failures: Ignored Solutions and Missed Opportunities

In the early 2020s, numerous **reports** and **think tanks**, including the **International Labour Organisation** and the **IMF**, issued warnings about the potential consequences of rapid automation without adequate policy responses. Solutions were proposed, but most were **dismissed or underfunded**:

- **Universal Basic Income (UBI)**: Pilot programmes showed promise, but most governments dismissed UBI as economically unsustainable.
- **Reskilling and Upskilling Initiatives**: Though discussed, reskilling programmes lacked the necessary **scale and funding** to match the speed of job displacement.
- **AI Regulation and Job Protection**: Limited regulatory frameworks allowed corporations to adopt AI without considering long-term impacts on labour markets. Tax incentives for hiring human workers were proposed, but they were shelved in favour of corporate tax cuts that further incentivised automation.

In contrast, **countries that had invested early in reskilling and lifelong learning programmes**, like **Estonia** and

Rwanda, were better able to cushion the blow. Their citizens were equipped to transition into new AI-supported roles, demonstrating that **proactive policies** could have mitigated the worst effects of the crisis. However, most governments failed to act, reluctant to impose regulations on booming tech sectors for fear of stifling innovation.

Psychological Impact and Generational Struggles

As AI continued to displace millions, the **psychological toll** became undeniable. Formerly stable workers faced not only **financial uncertainty**, but also a **profound sense of displacement and loss of identity**. Rates of **depression, anxiety**, and other **mental health conditions** surged. With few job prospects, many individuals — especially older workers and those without advanced technical skills — felt left behind in an economy that no longer valued their contributions.

The crisis did not impact everyone equally. Some of the world's wealthiest cities, like **New York, London**, and **San Francisco**, saw **enormous wealth accumulation** for a select few, even as these cities lost large segments of their **white-collar jobs** to automation. At the same time, younger generations — especially recent graduates — faced even greater challenges. Entry-level positions, once seen as the first step in a career, were **increasingly automated**, leaving fewer opportunities for young people to gain their first professional experience.

Older professionals who had mastered AI tools became **supercharged** and **indispensable**, but **younger workers** were at a significant disadvantage. They lacked the **hands-on experience** employers valued and were viewed as **less efficient than machines**. This created a **generational divide**, with younger workers resenting the older generation for holding onto jobs, while they struggled to enter the workforce.

The Turning Point: Growing Displacement and Economic Instability

As AI adoption spread across more industries, **job displacement accelerated**. Middle-class jobs in **administration, customer service**, and **data analysis** were automated as AI systems advanced to handle more complex tasks. This displacement impacted **blue-collar** and **white-collar workers** alike, with many forced to accept **gig work** or **low-wage service roles** with little security or opportunity for advancement.

With fewer people earning stable incomes, **consumer demand plummeted**. Retail sales, housing markets, and consumer spending declined sharply, even as **technological advances continued**. Companies that had once thrived on AI-driven efficiencies began to face **declining revenues** and **overproduction**, revealing the **unsustainability** of the AI-led boom.

The AI Class War

As AI continued to reshape industries, its impact highlighted stark inequalities. The technology that once held such promise in **improving lives** had, in many cases, **widened the gap** between those who benefitted from AI and those who did not.

Transformative Benefits for Some

AI delivered unprecedented advancements in sectors like **healthcare, finance**, and **research**. For professionals who could integrate AI into their work — such as doctors, scientists, and financial analysts — AI became an invaluable tool, enhancing their capabilities and creating a class of **"supercharged professionals."** These professionals saw their value rise as they harnessed AI to deliver faster, more accurate results. Meanwhile, the companies and individuals that controlled AI technology reaped **enormous financial rewards**.

Rising Inequality and Intergenerational Conflict

The benefits of AI were disproportionately captured by **older, experienced professionals** who had the skills to integrate AI into their work. These workers became **indispensable** to their employers, further increasing their value. In contrast, younger workers struggled to enter the workforce, with many entry-level jobs being **automated** before they could even gain experience. This **widened the generational divide**, as older workers thrived while the younger generation was left behind, deepening **social and economic resentment**.

The rising inequality led to significant **societal tensions**. Protests and political movements emerged, calling for more **inclusive and equitable AI policies**. Public discourse increasingly framed the situation as an **"AI class war,"** representing not only a conflict between **economic elites and the broader working class**, but also between **older, established professionals** and **younger generations** struggling to enter the workforce.

Conclusion: From Promise to Peril

The **Great Displacement Crisis** began with the promise of AI as a tool to revolutionise industries, increase productivity, and improve living standards. However, **unchecked technological advancement** and **insufficient policy responses** concentrated wealth in the hands of a few, while the majority faced **economic ruin**. This crisis serves as a cautionary tale, underscoring the urgent need for **proactive policies** that prioritise equitable adaptation to technological change.

See Also

- 2008 Financial Crisis
- Great Depression
- AI Ethics and Regulation
- Automation and Employment
- Universal Basic Income

This fictional Wikipedia entry is bleak. It is extreme. Will it happen? I don't know. Can it happen? Yes.

The CDE Innovation Prism tells us that these trends are definitely possible

The wave of Cheaper/Better/Faster is already happening, unnoticed, around the world. From TikTok laying off hundreds of content moderators in Malaysia, to Chinese game developers reducing human illustrators, to Greek Viva Mobile needing hundreds fewer customer service agents, and the Texas Education Agency requiring 4,000 fewer exam graders, this is happening today and will accelerate. Remember unbundling, then rebundling: each startup that discovers a role AI can perform cheaper, better, or faster will rapidly scale it across hundreds, even thousands, of companies worldwide.

The Supercharged (Enhancing) professionals and companies are also quickly emerging as AI tools enable individuals to achieve in days what once took months; for example, I leveraged AI to write this book in just 10% of the usual time. A friend of mine is having this crazy dream of launching a bank with only five employees, relying on AI-driven processes to handle tasks that traditionally required entire teams. AI is becoming the ultimate enhancer, allowing individuals and small teams to achieve extraordinary results and giving companies the ability to punch far above their weight.

The groundbreaking innovations (Different) are also happening in front of our eyes. From self-driving cars to real-time monitoring of baby's health to finding new drugs at a fraction of the cost, AI is already revolutionising our world and solving problems which we thought were impossible to solve.

II. AI and the Possibility of Collective Abundance

In **1879**, when **Thomas Edison** first demonstrated the electric light bulb, people may not have been able to predict every way in which electricity would transform the world. But what they could foresee was that the **abundance of energy** would unlock incredible possibilities for society. Over the decades that followed, electricity revolutionised industries, daily life, and economic opportunities by automating manual tasks and democratising access to power.

- Factories began operating more efficiently, running 24/7 to increase productivity.
- Homes and cities lit up, enabling longer working hours, safer streets, and better quality of life.
- New industries like telecommunications and mass media emerged, sparking waves of innovation and creating millions of jobs that had never existed before.

Electricity didn't just transform the economy — it transformed how we live and work. It gave us the tools to solve complex challenges, to be more productive, and to innovate in ways that were unimaginable before.

The same kind of **collective abundance** is possible today with **Artificial Intelligence**. Just as electricity automated physical tasks, AI is automating intellectual tasks, giving us access to a new source of power — cognitive power — that can change the way we work, think, and solve problems. AI's potential for abundance is clear:

- **Cognitive resources** that can help us make better decisions, solve problems faster, and unlock innovations across industries.
- Automation of routine intellectual tasks, allowing us to focus on creativity and strategy.
- Access to decision-making power, no longer limited to the few, but democratised through AI tools available to businesses, individuals, and governments alike.

But even more than these use cases, AI can potentially bring **unimaginable resources** to solve the world's biggest issues: Global Warming. Hunger. Water Scarcity. Health. Education.

Just like the abundance of energy from electricity powered industrial progress, AI's cognitive abundance has the potential to create a future of collective prosperity, where everyone benefits from its capabilities. AI can solve some of our biggest challenges, increase human potential, and transform industries for greater societal benefits.

But for this to happen, we need to ensure that **AI's abundance is collective**, not concentrated in the hands of a few.

The Threat of Passivity: Why Collective Abundance Won't Happen if We're Passive

If we're not careful, this abundance will not be shared. We know the trends: without intervention, the wealth and power created by AI will be concentrated among a small number of tech companies and elite individuals, while many others will be left behind.

- AI companies are pushing forward with massive investments, continually expanding their reach and power.
- Corporations are adopting AI to boost profits, cutting jobs, and increasing automation to stay competitive.
- Meanwhile, many workers are either either unaware or feel powerless to push back against these forces.
- If we remain passive spectators, the outcome is clear: AI's abundance will be concentrated in the hands of those who control the technology, leaving most people with less opportunity and more uncertainty.

Why Are We Passive?

So why are we **passive** in the face of such a profound transformation? There are several reasons:

1. **Complexity**: AI seems too complex for most people to engage with. It feels like something only technologists and engineers can understand or influence.

2. **Trust in Institutions**: Many of us assume that governments or big tech companies will manage AI responsibly. We trust that someone else will take care of it, leading to complacency.

3. **Overwhelmed by Scale**: The scale of AI's impact can feel overwhelming. People think their individual actions won't make a difference in the face of such a massive change.

4. **Assumption of Continuity**: We assume that the status quo will hold, believing that AI won't disrupt our lives significantly, at least not in the near future.

But being passive is a mistake. When we are passive, we leave the future of AI in the hands of a small elite — primarily tech companies and engineers — whose goals may not always align with the common good.

How We Can Shift from Passivity to Active Participation

We can't afford to remain passive. We must become active participants in shaping the future of AI, ensuring that it leads to collective abundance. To do this, we need to shift our perspective — just as we've done before.

A few decades ago, my grandfather's brother visited us from Vietnam. It was his first time in France, and we were excited to show him everything we loved. Crepes? He adored them! Onion soup with cheese? He couldn't understand how anyone could eat such a thing!

But what stands out most in my memory is our trip to the supermarket. As we checked out, the cashier handed us a plastic bag for our groceries. He was amazed. "Why didn't you bring a bag?" he asked. "What will you do with this plastic one? Just throw it away and get another next time?"

I explained that, as a wealthy society, we enjoyed the convenience of disposable bags, with no need to reuse them.

We rarely question why we do what we do — it would be exhausting to challenge everything we do.

Twenty years ago, our lens was tinted by the promises of consumerism, with little regard for sustainability. Back then, I never thought twice about using a new plastic bag every time I shopped.

With AI, it's crucial to recognise which lens we're using to project our future with this technology.

Take a moment to consider your lens on AI. Do you see it as an unstoppable part of progress? A force for good? A potential threat?

From my many discussions, AI is usually viewed as an inevitable force, one that will bring tremendous benefits. But also negative impacts, which we can't necessarily avoid.

AI's progress feels like a natural evolution, promising advancements in healthcare, education, and productivity, while also introducing issues like job displacement, privacy concerns, and ethical complexities.

Just as we once accepted consumerism at all cost, now we embrace AI as an unstoppable force — rarely pausing to consider the full scope of its implications.

Just as we've learned to put the planet at the centre of our thinking, we need the same kind of mindset shift when it comes to **AI**. In particular, we now need to put **humans at the centre of our thinking** in this new era of AI. It's time to consider how AI will affect people — how it will displace workers, redefine jobs, and shape society — and act accordingly.

This shift in thinking is critical. At CFTE, our motto is: **"In a tech world, we bet on people."** And that's the mindset we need for AI. AI is a tool — a powerful one — but it's a tool that should be used to enhance human potential, not just to drive profits or efficiency.

Becoming Active Actors: How We Can Shape AI's Future

So how can we be **active actors** rather than passive spectators? Here's how:

- **Policymakers** need to be proactive in creating regulations that ensure AI's benefits are distributed fairly, not just captured by a few tech giants. They should focus on reskilling workers, ensuring data privacy, and making AI accessible to all.
- **Businesses** must commit to using AI ethically. This means investing in human-AI collaboration, not just replacing workers with automation. It means reskilling employees to thrive in an AI-driven world and ensuring that AI is used to augment human capabilities, not replace them.
- **Individuals** need to engage with AI — not fear it, but understand it and use it. We need to push for ethical AI, advocate for fair policies, and work to ensure that AI is used to solve societal challenges, not just to increase corporate profits.

Conclusion: A New Perspective on AI for Collective Abundance

The future of AI is still ours to shape, but only if we act. Just as we've shifted our thinking to prioritise the planet, we need to shift our thinking to prioritise humans in this new AI-powered world. AI's abundance can bring incredible benefits to all of us, but only if we make it collective abundance — only if we ensure that everyone has a stake in this new future.

The choices we make today — whether we remain passive or become active participants — will determine whether AI empowers everyone or whether its benefits are concentrated in the hands of a few.

In the next section, I highlight different strategies for **individuals** (all of us, whoever we are), **policymakers** (those who can shape society) and **industry leaders** (those who can shape business) to help us shape AI to benefit us, humans. You might find some suggestions very useful, or disagree with some of them, and it's totally fine. We will not reach collective abundance through a single point of view – we need a diversity of perspectives which is as broad as possible. So consider these ideas as a starting point for your own reflection.

Individuals: Thriving in an AI World and Shaping Collective Abundance

As an individual in an AI-driven world, your goal is twofold: **first, to do well** in this rapidly changing landscape by understanding how AI is transforming work and preparing for those changes. **Second, to help shape** the future of AI so that it leads to **collective abundance**, benefiting not just a few, but society as a whole.

Doing Well in an AI World

The Impact of AI on Jobs: Understanding the Big Picture

AI is creating **three key trends** in the job market: **mass displacement**, **supercharged professionals**, and **creative disruptors**. Understanding these trends can help you identify where your job fits and what steps you need to take to thrive.

- **Mass Displacement**: AI is automating many repetitive tasks, leading to job losses in sectors like customer service, manufacturing, and administration. Jobs that involve routine work — such as data entry or basic customer interactions — are increasingly being done by AI systems.
- **Supercharged Professionals**: AI won't eliminate all jobs. In many industries, AI will augment roles, helping professionals become more productive by automating repetitive tasks and offering insights that improve decision-making. For example, marketers, healthcare professionals, and engineers will use AI tools to supercharge their work.
- **Creative Disruptors**: A small number of people and companies will use AI to create entirely new industries and business models. Think of AI pioneers like the team behind ChatGPT or AlphaFold, who are transforming the fields of language models and biology.

> **Key Message**: The most practical goal for most individuals is to become a **supercharged professional** — someone who leverages AI to enhance their role. This requires **leveraging** AI and positioning yourself for opportunities that arise as your job evolves.

Identifying Future-Proof Jobs by Thinking Like AI

The best way to predict how AI will impact your job is to look at it from the **perspective of AI**. AI's disruption starts with specific **use cases** that prove successful in one industry and then spread across similar sectors. By understanding where AI is already making an impact, you can anticipate how it will affect your role and industry.

- **AI's Expansion of Proven Use Cases**:

  - AI doesn't disrupt randomly. It starts by solving problems where it provides the most value. Once AI proves effective in one area, it scales across industries. For example, OpenAI's chatbot at Klarna handles customer queries efficiently, signalling that routine customer service roles across other industries (like banking, retail, and e-commerce) will likely follow this trend.

- **Job Displacement and Evolution**:

  - Roles in customer service, administration, and routine tasks are at risk of displacement as AI takes over repetitive functions. However, this also means that new opportunities are emerging for those willing to adapt. Customer service roles are evolving into high-touch, specialised roles where professionals manage complex customer interactions that AI cannot handle.

  - Additionally, AI is creating new jobs — like AI monitors, AI trainers, and quality control specialists — to oversee, train, and manage the AI systems themselves.

281

- **Supercharged Roles and New Opportunities**:

  - As AI automates routine tasks, there will be fewer traditional customer service agents, but the remaining ones will be supercharged — using AI tools to deliver high-touch services and solve complex problems. These professionals will need to understand how to work with AI to manage and enhance customer experiences.

  - New jobs will also emerge for AI trainers (people who fine-tune AI systems), AI monitors (who ensure that systems work correctly), and quality control specialists (who ensure that AI is providing accurate and ethical results).

Key Message: By thinking like AI — understanding where AI is already proving successful — you can anticipate which jobs are likely to be disrupted and where new opportunities are emerging. Don't focus on holding onto the same job. Instead, prepare to transition into **supercharged roles** or **new AI-driven jobs**.

Becoming a Supercharged Professional: The Three Core Components

The best way to future-proof your career is by becoming a supercharged professional. This means combining domain expertise, AI skills, and a lifelong learning mindset to stay relevant and competitive in an AI-driven world.

- **Domain Expertise:**

  Having deep knowledge of your field — whether it's finance, healthcare, education, or any other sector — is the foundation of becoming a supercharged professional. Your understanding of how the industry works, its best practices, and its challenges gives you the ability to apply AI effectively within that context.

Action Step: Continue building your industry-specific knowledge through experience, training, and staying up to date with trends.

- **AI and Technology Skills:**

  You don't need to be an AI developer, but you need to understand how to use AI tools that apply to your role. Whether it's automating workflows, using AI for data analysis, or leveraging AI to make better decisions, AI literacy is key to staying competitive.

  Action Step: Take courses on AI basics relevant to your industry. Learn how AI is used in your field and start integrating these tools into your daily work.

- **Lifelong Learning Mindset:**

  AI is driving rapid changes across industries. The most successful professionals are those who commit to lifelong learning and stay adaptable. Whether it's new AI tools, industry trends, or emerging skills, staying curious and open to learning will help you thrive.

  Action Step: Regularly invest time in learning — whether through formal courses, reading industry reports, attending webinars, or networking with peers.

Key Message: To thrive in an AI-driven world, you need to combine **domain expertise**, **AI literacy**, and a **lifelong learning mindset**. Becoming a **supercharged professional** means using AI to enhance your work and stay adaptable to ongoing changes.

Skills You Need to Thrive in an AI World (SHIME Framework)

While many people think of hard skills like coding or programming when they imagine thriving in an AI world, these are often misconceptions for the majority of professionals. That's where the **SHIME framework** comes in — covering **Soft skills**, **Hard skills**, **Industry knowledge**, **Mindset**, and **Experience**.

1. Soft Skills (S)

AI can't replace core human skills like communication, empathy, and collaboration. These soft skills will be increasingly valuable as AI automates routine tasks.

- **Communication**: AI can handle data processing, but humans will still need to communicate complex ideas, strategies, and emotional insights to clients and teams.
- **Collaboration**: Working with others — both humans and AI — will be crucial for solving complex problems in a technology-driven workplace.
- **Emotional Intelligence**: Understanding emotions and maintaining human connections in an AI world will be key to leading teams and building relationships.

2. Hard Skills (H)

While you don't need to become an AI engineer, AI literacy and data skills will help you use AI tools effectively.

- **AI Literacy**: Understand the basics of AI and how it applies to your field.
- **Data Literacy**: Learn to interpret data and use data-driven decision-making.
- **Adaptability to New Technologies**: Be open to adopting new AI tools as they become available.

3. Industry Knowledge (I)

Having deep domain expertise is essential. AI enhances roles, but your industry-specific knowledge allows you to apply AI effectively.

- **Stay Current with Trends**: Keep up with how AI is transforming your industry.

- **Leverage Your Expertise**: Use your industry knowledge to guide AI implementation in ways that provide real value.

4. Mindset (M)

A growth mindset and a commitment to lifelong learning will help you stay adaptable as AI continues to evolve.

- **Lifelong Learning**: Keep learning and stay curious about new trends, tools, and skills.
- **Adaptability**: Be open to change, experiment with new AI tools, and view challenges as opportunities for growth.

5. Experience (E)

As knowledge becomes commoditised with AI, real-life experience becomes much more valuable, and it could be acquired in many ways.

- **On the job experience** can be acquired in the course of a job, but also internships, projects, contracts – the world of work is much more varied than before.
- **Experiential and practical training** are new ways to acquire hands-on experience that are valuable when on the job experience is limited.

There are dozens of different skills in the SHIME framework, and those mentioned are only an illustration to help think about the breadth of skills that can help to thrive in an AI world.

Key Message of SHIME: Thriving in an AI world isn't just about hard skills like coding. You need a broader set of skills — **Soft skills**, **Hard skills**, **Industry knowledge**, **Mindset**, and **Experience** — to truly excel as a user of AI.

Helping Shape AI for Collective Abundance

Why Collective Abundance Won't Happen if We're Passive

If individuals remain passive, AI's benefits will be concentrated in the hands of a few. We've seen how AI companies, driven by profit motives, push forward with automation, while society grapples with the consequences.

Why We're Passive:

- **Complexity**: AI seems too complex for many people to engage with meaningfully.
- **Trust in Institutions**: People assume governments or companies will handle AI's development responsibly.
- **False Sense of Security**: Many believe that AI won't personally affect them in the near future.

How to Be an Active Participant: Small Actions for Big Impact

Being an active participant doesn't require becoming an AI expert. Here's how you can help shape AI for **collective abundance**:

- **Change Your Mindset**: Like me who didn't consider the environmental impact of plastics when I talked to my grandfather's brother, we now need to place **humans at the centre** of AI. The CFTE motto — **"In a tech world, we bet on people"** — captures this shift. AI should serve people, not just profit.

- **Speak Up in Your Workplace**: Ask how AI is being implemented, raise questions about ethical use, and encourage transparency around AI decisions.

- **Engage in Public Conversations**: Comment on posts, join discussions, or share articles about AI and its societal

286

impacts. Your voice matters in shaping how AI is viewed and implemented.

Conclusion: Thriving and Shaping the Future

To succeed in an AI-driven world, individuals must focus on becoming **supercharged professionals** — leveraging AI to enhance their roles and staying adaptable through lifelong learning. At the same time, it's critical to take an active role in shaping AI's future for the collective good by speaking up, engaging with AI discussions, and ensuring that humans remain central to AI's development.

Policymakers: Harnessing AI's Potential and Shaping Society's Future

Introduction: AI's Huge Potential and the Policymaker's Role

AI is one of the most transformative forces shaping the future of our economy and society. Its potential is enormous — AI can revolutionise healthcare, speeding up diagnoses and personalising treatments; it can transform education, providing personalised learning experiences; and it can optimise industries, driving new levels of efficiency and creativity. The promise of AI is a future where innovation solves problems once considered impossible, where economies grow, and where people live better, healthier lives.

But with this vast potential comes a responsibility: ensuring that society as a whole benefits from AI, not just a select few. For policymakers, this means being deeply engaged in AI discussions and shaping the technology's trajectory. To do this effectively, they must be on the same level of understanding as the CEOs of AI companies and large organisations. AI isn't just about technology — it's about reshaping industries, transforming job markets, and redefining human roles in the workforce. Policymakers need to be as fluent in AI's impacts and possibilities as the leaders driving its development. Only by having this level of AI literacy can policymakers ensure that the benefits of AI reach everyone, and that society remains resilient in the face of profound technological change.

Anticipating, Managing Impact, and Shaping AI's Direction

Understanding AI's Impact on Jobs and Society

AI's disruptive impact on jobs and society is profound. For policymakers, it's about **anticipating** these changes and **shaping the direction** AI takes to ensure that it leads to

288

inclusive growth. AI's impact can be broken down into three key trends:

- **Mass Displacement**: AI is already automating routine tasks in industries like customer service, manufacturing, and administration, leading to the displacement of millions of jobs. These workers must be reskilled or transition into new roles.
- **Supercharged Professionals**: AI will also enhance certain jobs, creating a new class of supercharged professionals. These are roles where AI augments human capabilities — such as healthcare professionals using AI for diagnostics or marketers leveraging AI for data-driven insights.
- **Creative Disruptors**: A small group of creative disruptors will reshape entire industries by building new AI-powered solutions. These are the innovators who will create jobs and opportunities in sectors that don't yet exist.

Policymakers' Role: Beyond managing these impacts, policymakers need to shape the direction of AI so that it becomes a force for collective good. This includes encouraging the use of AI to address society's biggest challenges, from climate change to public health. By shaping how AI is deployed, policymakers can ensure that it doesn't just optimise existing systems but creates new pathways for solving global problems.

Policymakers' Dual Role: Anticipating and Shaping the Future

Policymakers must do more than just respond to AI's disruptions — they need to **actively shape** its future. This involves two critical areas of responsibility:

Anticipating AI's Impact on Jobs and Society:

- **Education and Reskilling**: Policymakers need to redesign education systems to prepare workers for the AI economy. This includes not just **children and student education**, but also **continuous learning** — something most countries

289

currently lack. Given that people will work for 40+ years, it's essential to have systems in place to help them **reskill** and **upskill** throughout their careers. Policymakers must ensure that education isn't just for children but for adults too.

- **Economic Stability**: Prepare for potential economic shocks caused by mass job displacement. This could involve piloting programs like universal basic income (UBI) or expanding social safety nets to support those displaced by automation.

Shaping AI's Direction:

- **Steering AI towards societal good**: Policymakers should incentivise the development of AI solutions that solve global challenges. Public investment, tax breaks, and public-private partnerships should be directed toward AI initiatives that address healthcare, education, and environmental sustainability.

- **Proactively Addressing Inequality**: AI is poised to create unprecedented economic opportunities, but also risks widening the gap between those who benefit from AI and those left behind. Policymakers need to ensure that AI's benefits are distributed equitably, providing AI education and access to AI tools for underserved communities, ensuring that the digital divide doesn't deepen.

Key Message: Policymakers must be able to **anticipate AI's impact** while also **shaping its future**. By directing AI towards **public good** and ensuring that education and economic policies support **inclusive growth**, they can steer society toward a future of **collective abundance**.

Rethinking Systems and Creating Regulatory Frameworks for AI

Regulatory Frameworks: The Need for Expertise in the Public Sector

In industries that are critical to society — like finance or healthcare — governments have established strong regulatory frameworks to ensure the public good. These frameworks also come with a crucial advantage: they build deep expertise within the public sector, creating regulators who are knowledgeable and able to ensure that industries serve society's best interests.

However, in the field of technology — which is arguably the most impactful industry in today's world — such regulatory expertise is often lacking. For instance, when CrowdStrike went down, it caused widespread disruption: airplanes were grounded, and bank payments were halted. This shows how much society relies on technology, yet most countries lack a regulatory body with the deep technical expertise to understand and manage the complexities of technology. This gap in knowledge and oversight poses risks for society, particularly as AI becomes more integrated into critical infrastructure.

- **Regulatory Frameworks for Technology**: Policymakers might create AI-specific regulatory bodies that focus on ethical AI, data privacy, and system resilience. These regulators should not only set rules but also develop deep expertise in AI to ensure the technology is being used responsibly and for societal good.
- **The Role of Humans at the Centre**: Beyond regulating AI itself, policymakers should ensure that human interests remain at the centre of AI development. This means establishing accountability for the impacts AI has on employment and society. For example, if mass displacement occurs across sectors, who is responsible for making sure people are reskilled?

- Governments could designate an agency or task force responsible for mass displacement across sectors and ensuring that displaced workers are supported with reskilling programs.
- In many countries, education systems focus heavily on children and universities but neglect continuous education for adults, despite the fact that people are working for 40+ years. Policymakers must create systems that support lifelong learning and continuous skills development.

Key Message: Just as finance and healthcare are regulated to protect the public good, **technology** — and especially AI — needs a **regulatory framework** to ensure that it operates responsibly and with the necessary **public oversight**. Policymakers must ensure that **humans are at the centre** of AI development, with clear systems for **reskilling** and **lifelong learning.**

Being an Active Actor: Shaping AI's Future

Policymakers have the responsibility not only to regulate but also to actively shape how AI impacts society. This requires proactive leadership and a vision for how AI can drive societal progress. Rather than simply reacting to AI's effects, policymakers should lead the conversation on how AI can solve societal problems and create inclusive growth.

- **Proactive Leadership in AI Innovation**: Policymakers must be at the forefront of global AI discussions, shaping international AI frameworks to ensure ethical use, data privacy, and inclusive growth. This is critical not just for national policy but for global leadership, as AI knows no borders and its impact is international.

- **Investing in AI for Public Good**: Governments can drive AI innovation that benefits society by providing incentives for companies developing ethical AI solutions. For instance, offering tax breaks and public funding for AI initiatives that tackle global healthcare issues, education inequality, or climate change can steer AI development in a direction that benefits everyone.

Key Message: Policymakers must take a **proactive role** in shaping the future of AI. This means leading global discussions on **ethical AI**, creating systems that protect **human interests**, and investing in AI-driven solutions that solve **global challenges** and create **inclusive growth**.

Conclusion: Balancing Risk Mitigation with Collective Abundance

Policymakers are uniquely positioned to manage the risks of AI while harnessing its potential for collective good. By anticipating disruption, reshaping regulatory frameworks, and actively driving AI innovation for the public good, they can create a future where AI serves everyone, not just a privileged few. To do this effectively, they must be as knowledgeable about AI as the leaders of AI companies themselves — ensuring that human interests are at the centre of AI development.

Policymakers who approach AI with a **deep understanding** and a **vision for the future** will be **leaders** guiding society through the greatest transformation of our time.

Industry Leaders: Maximising AI for Sustainable Growth and Innovation

Introduction: AI as a Tool for Sustainable Growth, Not Just Cost-Cutting

AI presents a powerful opportunity to improve the bottom line, primarily by cutting costs through automation and replacing human workers with AI systems. Many companies will take this approach, reducing their workforce in favour of AI-driven efficiencies. But as any CEO knows, cost-cutting alone is rarely a recipe for sustainable growth. While cost reductions may improve margins in the short term, true long-term success depends on growing the top line by innovating, creating new products, and entering new markets.

This is where the right approach to AI comes in. The real opportunity with AI is not just in reducing costs but in unlocking innovation, supercharging your workforce, and empowering creative disruptors who will transform industries. Companies that leverage AI to drive new products, faster development cycles, and breakthroughs — like Moderna, which uses AI to accelerate drug development, or AlphaFold, which is revolutionising biology — are setting themselves up for sustainable success.

For industry leaders, the challenge is to balance the immediate gains from AI-driven automation with the long-term benefits of using AI to drive innovation. This means thinking beyond cost-cutting and focusing on how AI can supercharge people, open new opportunities, and drive business growth.

Leveraging AI for Business Success and Long-Term Growth

AI as a Cost-Cutting Tool vs. Long-Term Growth Strategy

Goal: Understand the appeal of **cost-cutting** but balance it with the importance of **innovation** and **long-term growth** for sustainable success.

- **AI and Cost-Cutting**: AI offers immediate gains through automation by reducing the need for human labour. This leads to lower operational costs, especially in roles involving repetitive tasks like customer service, manufacturing, and data processing.
- **The Risks of Over-Automation**: However, relying solely on AI to replace human jobs can have long-term risks:
- **Innovation Stagnation**: Over-focusing on cost-cutting can lead to a loss of **innovation**. AI can optimise, but it cannot **create new ideas** like humans can.
- **Talent and Customer Loss**: If companies lose the human touch, they risk alienating customers and having trouble attracting and retaining top talent who thrive in innovative environments.
- **Balancing Cost-Cutting with Growth**: While cost-cutting may improve short-term profits, the true power of AI lies in growing the top line — by enabling businesses to innovate, create new products, and improve existing processes.

Key Message: AI should not just be used for **cost-cutting**. Industry leaders must focus on using AI to **drive growth**, ensuring that their businesses stay **innovative** and **competitive** in the long term.

AI as an Innovation Driver: Leveraging Creative Disruptors to Fuel Growth

Goal: See AI as a catalyst for innovation and long-term growth, using it to drive new product development, accelerate processes, and tap into the breakthroughs of creative disruptors.

- **AI and Innovation**: AI has the potential to unlock new products, services, and business models by enabling faster and more accurate data analysis, trend forecasting, and development cycles. Rather than focusing solely on cutting costs, leaders should use AI to innovate faster, bringing new offerings to market ahead of competitors.

Example — Moderna: Moderna has used AI to accelerate drug development by speeding up the discovery and testing processes. What would normally take years can now be achieved in months, positioning Moderna at the forefront of pharmaceutical innovation.

- **Leveraging Creative Disruptors**: AI breakthroughs from creative disruptors, such as the development of AlphaFold, show how AI can revolutionise industries by solving problems previously thought unsolvable. AlphaFold's success in predicting protein structures is a breakthrough that could reshape biological research and drug discovery — and companies like Moderna are already leveraging it to accelerate their own innovations.

  Moderna and AlphaFold: By combining in-house AI capabilities with external breakthroughs like **AlphaFold**, Moderna can stay ahead of competitors, significantly reducing the time it takes to bring new drugs to market, while solving complex biological challenges.

- **Supercharging People with AI**: AI should also be used to augment human capabilities, turning employees into supercharged professionals. Rather than replacing people, companies can use AI tools to enable workers to make smarter decisions, increase productivity, and innovate faster.

  Example — AI in Marketing: AI tools can help marketers **analyse customer data** and predict trends more accurately, allowing them to create **personalised campaigns** and **launch products faster**. By supercharging marketers with AI, companies can tap into **creativity** while leveraging the efficiency of AI.

Key Message: AI is a powerful tool for **innovation**. Industry leaders should use AI to drive **new product development**, leverage **creative disruptors** like **AlphaFold**, and

---

> **supercharge their people** to stay competitive and create **long-term value.**

Leading Responsibly and Shaping AI for Societal Benefit

The Ethical Responsibility of AI Adoption

Goal: Recognise the **moral responsibility** that industry leaders have to ensure that AI benefits both their business and society.

- **Responsible AI Adoption**: AI must be implemented ethically, with careful consideration of its impact on employees, customers, and society. Leaders must avoid AI systems that are biased or infringe on privacy and data protection.

  Avoiding Bias: AI systems must be transparent and fair, ensuring that they do not perpetuate biases in hiring, promotions, or customer interactions.

- **Ensuring Workforce Well-Being**: Leaders have a responsibility to help workers who may be displaced by AI. This means investing in reskilling and upskilling programs that help employees transition into new roles.
  Reskilling Programs: Companies must create systems to retrain workers for roles that involve managing AI systems, ensuring that employees can thrive alongside AI rather than being replaced by it.

> **Key Message**: Industry leaders have a **responsibility** to adopt AI ethically, ensuring that it benefits society, protects **privacy**, and helps workers transition into new, AI-enhanced roles.

AI for Solving Global Challenges: Driving Collective Abundance

Goal: Use AI to solve societal challenges, contributing to both business success and collective well-being.

- **AI for Global Good**: AI has the potential to tackle global challenges like climate change, healthcare inequality, and education gaps. Businesses that leverage AI for these challenges not only do good but also create new market opportunities and long-term business sustainability.
  Example — AI for Climate Change: AI can be used to optimise energy consumption, reduce waste, and improve supply chain efficiencies — helping companies reduce their environmental footprint while also saving costs.
- **Aligning Business with Societal Good**: Companies that focus on solving real-world problems with AI can create long-term partnerships with governments and gain regulatory incentives. This approach ensures that AI-driven growth benefits society as a whole and enhances corporate reputation.

Key Message: AI can be a powerful tool for **solving global problems**. Industry leaders should align their AI strategies with the goal of creating **collective abundance**, benefiting both business and society.

Preparing the Workforce for the AI-Driven Future

Reskilling and Upskilling Workers for AI

Goal: Recognise the role of industry leaders to prepare their workforce for the future by investing in **continuous learning** and **upskilling** programs.

- **Investing in Training Programs**: Leaders must provide employees with the skills they need to work alongside AI. This includes offering reskilling opportunities for workers whose roles are being automated and upskilling for those who need to learn new AI-enhanced tools.

Internal Training Programs: Develop internal programs that help workers transition into AI-enhanced roles, such as AI system managers, data analysts, or roles that require collaboration with AI tools.

- **Creating a Lifelong Learning Culture**: AI and technology are evolving rapidly, and businesses need to create a culture where employees are encouraged to engage in lifelong learning. Providing access to online courses, workshops, and mentorship programs can help employees stay up to date with the latest developments in AI.

Key Message: Leaders must prepare their workforce for the **AI-driven future** by investing in **reskilling** and **upskilling**, ensuring that employees can thrive alongside AI and contribute to the company's success.

Conclusion: The Time to Shape AI's Future is Now

I hope you've enjoyed this journey with me as we explored the AI-fication of jobs and its broader impact on society. The transformation driven by AI is not some abstract future — it's happening now, and it's happening fast. AI touches the core of who we are, impacting not just our work but our very identity as human beings. **Jobs** are not just tasks — they're expressions of our skills, our creativity, and, for many of us, our purpose. So when we talk about AI's impact on jobs, we're not just talking about **economics** — we're talking about **human lives**.

It's natural to feel the weight of the question: Will AI take my job? Replace me? Leave me behind? Create new jobs? But this question, though important, is not enough. It **limits our thinking** to the role of the disrupted. Instead, we need to take control of the narrative, to **shift our perspective**. Instead of asking how AI will change us, we must ask: **How will we change AI?**

That's why we turned the lens around in this book. We examined AI **not from the perspective of the incumbent** — us, the workers, the employees — but from the **disruptor's viewpoint**. By understanding AI's impact through the CDE Innovation Prism, we identified the patterns for jobs in an AI world: mass displacement, the rise of supercharged professionals, and the emergence of creative disruptors. These trends are real, and the momentum behind them is undeniable.

The Forces We Face and the Role We Must Play

Make no mistake: AI companies are incredibly well-funded and racing toward ever more capable systems. Businesses everywhere are seizing these technologies to drive efficiency, reduce costs, and boost profits. These are the realities — and they put us, the people, in a precarious position. As employees and individuals, we're often the **incumbents** being disrupted, while others — corporations and tech developers — stand to benefit.

But this is not the inevitable story of AI. We **do not have to accept** a future where AI benefits only a privileged few while the rest of us are left behind. The future is not set. And if we want a different outcome, we need to act now. We need to stop being passive spectators and become active participants in this transformation.

Shifting Our Mindset: From Spectators to Active Participants

This book has been about showing the path to empowerment. For individuals, it means embracing the role of the **supercharged professional**, using AI to enhance your own work and seize the opportunities it creates. It's about understanding AI, upskilling, and **positioning yourself** not just to survive in an AI world, but to thrive in it.

For policymakers, it's about **leading from the front —** being **at the table** in AI discussions, driving the rules and regulations that will shape AI's ethical use, and ensuring **AI benefits everyone**. **Education reform**, **reskilling programs**, and **AI regulation** are not optional; they are the essential tools for shaping a future where technology serves society, not the other way around.

And for industry leaders, it's about **transforming organisations** through people, not despite them. AI should not be a means to cut headcount — it should be a tool for **empowering your workforce**, **driving innovation**, and creating a more dynamic, more human-centric future.

Be Activists for Humanity

But beyond these roles, there's a responsibility that rests on all of us. We must be **activists for humanity**. In a world increasingly dominated by technology, we must make sure that **people remain central** to every decision made about AI. It's time we put human well-being, equality, and dignity at the forefront of AI development. As I've said before, **AI is too important to be left to the technologists alone**. It's about more than algorithms and profits — it's about shaping a future where AI enhances human potential.

A Message of Urgency and Hope

This book began with a warning about the **cost of inaction** — but it's also a message of **hope**. We are living in an age where the **impossible becomes possible**. The very technology that threatens to disrupt can also be the key to unlocking collective abundance — a world where the benefits of AI are shared by all. But reaching this future requires **bold action**. It requires us to seize this moment and recognise that we each have the power to shape what comes next.

With AI advancing at exponential speed, the timing of our actions is critical. Unlike past technologies, its capabilities are progressing on a weekly basis, demanding swift adaptation. Every decision we make shapes a future that may look vastly different even a year from now.

Just as **creative disruptors** will reshape industries, each one of us can have an **outsized impact** on how AI shapes our world. We don't need to be AI experts to make a difference. We need to be **informed**, **engaged**, and **willing to speak up** — in our workplaces, in our communities, and in the halls of power.

The Time to Act is Now: Be Part of This Journey

I urge you to take this journey further. Be part of the conversation, be part of the solution. AI is not a future that's being handed to us — it's a future we are all helping to create. Whether as individuals embracing AI, policymakers driving the rules of engagement, or business leaders innovating through AI, we all have a **responsibility** to shape AI so that it **benefits us all**.

The time to act is now. The future of AI is being written today. Don't just stand by — be part of the journey. **Together, we can ensure that AI leads to collective abundance**, a future where technology serves humanity, elevates our potential, and creates a more equitable, prosperous world for all.

"If not me, then who? If not now, then when?"

Arnold Schwarzenegger (amongst others...)

A bias towards action

If you've reached this point and found the ideas in this book compelling — whether about becoming "supercharged," contributing thoughtfully to AI discussions, or advocating for a human-centred approach to AI — you may be asking yourself, "What next?". And with AI advancing at breakneck speed, there's no time to waste. Every step taken today helps us stay proactive in a world that could look very different within just a year.

The aim of *The AI-fication of Jobs* is not only to provide insights but also to inspire each of us, at every level, to become active drivers of change. No matter your role, you have the power to make a difference — beginning with your own actions and decisions.

To support this journey, I have developed a Resource Page that offers links to valuable websites, tools, and templates to help you put these ideas into practice. For instance, you'll find information about AI literacy, templates for applying the CDE Prism framework, as well as links to additional reading and research focused on AI and the future of work.

Another way to make an impact is by sharing this book and its ideas with colleagues, leaders, and others in your network. By encouraging broader conversations around the responsible, human-centred use of AI, you can help expand awareness and inspire others to take meaningful actions of their own.

Consider taking even the smallest steps forward — whether that's exploring topics that resonate with you, beginning a conversation in your workplace, or reflecting on how you might apply these ideas personally.

The path to a responsible, human-centred AI future begins here and now, with each of us. Thank you for joining this journey.

Link to Resource Page:
https://courses.cfte.education/aification

References

ADP Research Institute. (2024). Global Workforce View: The AI Shift in the Modern Workplace. ADP.

Bank for International Settlements. (1966). Recent innovations in international banking (No. 1). Retrieved from https://fraser.stlouisfed.org/files/docs/meltzer/cenlon66.pdf

Bardini, T. (2000). Bootstrapping: Douglas Engelbart, Coevolution, and the Origins of Personal Computing. Stanford University Press.

Bessen, J. (2019). AI and Jobs: The Role of Demand. National Bureau of Economic Research.

BBC News. (2024, February 9). World's first year-long breach of key 1.5C warming limit. https://www.bbc.com/news/science-environment-68110310

Board of Governors of the Federal Reserve System (U.S.). (1966). The Current Economic Position and Prospects (Paper presented by the Central Bank of London). Retrieved from https://fraser.stlouisfed.org/files/docs/meltzer/cenlon66.pdf

Chancel, L., & Piketty, T. (2021). Global income inequality, 1820–2020: The persistence and mutation of extreme inequality. Journal of the European Economic Association, 19(6), 3025–3060. Retrieved from http://www.piketty.pse.ens.fr/files/ChancelPiketty2021JEEA.pdf

Christensen, C. M. (1997). The Innovator's Dilemma: When New Technologies Cause Great Firms to Fail. Harvard Business Review Press.

Christensen, C. M., Hall, T., Dillon, K., & Duncan, D. S. (2016). Competing Against Luck: The Story of Innovation and Customer Choice. Harper Business.

DeepMind. (2024). AlphaFold 2 and the Future of Drug Discovery. DeepMind Report.

Gartner, Inc. (n.d.). Gartner Hype Cycle. Gartner Research.

Henderson, R. M., & Clark, K. B. (1990). Architectural Innovation: The Reconfiguration of Existing Product Technologies and the Failure of Established Firms. Administrative Science Quarterly, 35(1), 9-30.

International Monetary Fund. (2023). World Economic Outlook: The Digital Economy and AI's Impact on Labor Markets. IMF Publishing.

Jumper, J., et al. (2021). Highly Accurate Protein Structure Prediction with AlphaFold. Nature, 596, 583-589.

Kelly, J. (2024, March 4). Klarna's AI Assistant is Doing the Job of 700 Workers, Company Says. Forbes. Retrieved from https://www.forbes.com/sites/jackkelly/2024/03/04/klarnas-ai-assistant-is-doing-the-job-of-700-workers-company-says/.

Kim, W. C., & Mauborgne, R. (2005). Blue Ocean Strategy: How to Create Uncontested Market Space and Make Competition Irrelevant. Harvard Business Review Press.

Osterwalder, A., & Pigneur, Y. (2010). Business Model Generation: A Handbook for Visionaries, Game Changers, and Challengers. Wiley.

PwC. (2023). AI in Financial Services: A Catalyst for Transformation. PricewaterhouseCoopers.

Schwartz, P. (1991). The Art of the Long View: Planning for the Future in an Uncertain World. Doubleday.

Sinek, S. (2009). Start with Why: How Great Leaders Inspire Everyone to Take Action. Portfolio.

About the Author

Huy Nguyen Trieu is a trailblazer in finance, technology, and disruptive business models, renowned for his pioneering insights on Fintech and the future of work. His career spans entrepreneurship, senior banking roles, and academia, giving him a broad and unique perspective on how technology reshapes industries. As co-founder of CFTE (Centre for Finance, Technology, and Entrepreneurship), Huy brings together diverse voices from business, academia, policy, and entrepreneurship to prepare global leaders for a rapidly evolving economy.

 Huy's career has bridged many worlds, from senior roles at Citi and Royal Bank of Scotland, to CEO of the tech start-up Ukibi and Associate Fellow at Oxford Said Business School and Industry Fellow at Imperial College. Recognised as one of the earliest to analyse Fintech's transformative impact, Huy co-created the Oxford Fintech Programme and pioneering courses at Hong Kong University and Imperial College London, equipping hundreds of thousands of professionals with the tools to navigate a world of tech-driven finance.

As a founding partner of Supercharger, Asia's largest Fintech accelerator, Huy has helped start-ups innovate in one of the world's fastest-growing markets. His extensive global network spans regulators, policymakers, corporations, and start-ups across Europe, Asia, the Middle East, and the United States, giving him unmatched insight into the interplay between technology, business, and regulation.

Huy is a firm believer that a world driven by technology unlocks vast opportunities for individuals and society to thrive. To harness these possibilities fully, he emphasises the importance of including everyone in the conversation — from policymakers and business leaders to educators and citizens. Through his work, Huy champions an inclusive approach to the future of work, where technology becomes a force for shared progress and collective abundance.

About CFTE

CFTE Centre for Finance, Technology and Entrepreneurship

CFTE (Centre for Finance, Technology, and Entrepreneurship) is a global leader in education for finance and technology, dedicated to delivering world-class knowledge and skills at scale. With a mission to ensure that everyone, regardless of location or background, has access to cutting-edge learning, CFTE prepares individuals for success in a technology-driven world. Its motto, "In a tech-driven world, we bet on people," reflects its commitment to empowering individuals to thrive in the digital economy.

Through partnerships with governments, central banks, multinational corporations, and tech firms, CFTE offers a diverse range of learning experiences — from large-scale online courses to executive workshops.

By combining technology with insights into human behaviour, CFTE continually pushes the boundaries of effective upskilling for millions. It collaborates with industry leaders to produce influential research and insights, shaping a deeper understanding of the rapidly evolving intersections between technology, finance, and education.

Co-founded by Tram Anh Nguyen and Huy Nguyen Trieu, both passionate advocates of lifelong learning, CFTE brings together a global ecosystem of governments, regulators, businesses, and entrepreneurs, working together to drive meaningful impact in the future of education and work.

Printed in Dunstable, United Kingdom